BLACK & WHITE ARMY

A season supporting the Toon

BLACK & WHITE ARMY

Paul Brown

First published in Great Britain in 2003 by
The Breedon Books Publishing Company Limited
Breedon House, 3 The Parker Centre,
Derby, DE21 4SZ.

ISBN 1 85983 384 5

Printed and bound by Butler & Tanner,
Frome, Somerset, England.

Jacket printing by Lawrence-Allen Colour Printers,
Weston-super-Mare, Somerset, England.

Contents

Introduction	6
Chapter One – The Close Season	9
Chapter Two – The Pre-Season	18
Chapter Three – August	29
Chapter Four – September	42
Chapter Five – October	54
Chapter Six – November	64
Chapter Seven – December	76
Chapter Eight – January	90
Chapter Nine – February	102
Chapter Ten – March	117
Chapter Eleven – April	131
Chapter Twelve – May	141
Appendix	152
Index	156

Introduction

WE WERE talking about football, as we tend to do for the best part of every day of our lives. At home and at work, with friends and with strangers, when we're doing nothing and when we should be doing something else, in fanzines and on football phone-ins, via text message and by e-mail. This is the way of the football supporter.

It was shirtsleeves-warm, but then it always is in Newcastle upon Tyne. We sat in the beer garden of a Quayside pub, watched the sun sink over the famous Tyne Bridge, and decanted bottles of Newcastle Brown Ale into our glasses.

We were talking about Newcastle United Football Club. None of us around this table of friends had made a conscious decision to support Newcastle United. That honour had been bestowed upon us by virtue of being born, and growing up, here on Tyneside. We are Geordies. We are members of the Toon Army.

We were talking about our expectations for the forthcoming season, 2002-03. And we were talking about the remarkable journey our club had taken us on over recent years. Perhaps no other set of supporters had travelled on such an emotional roller coaster ride as the devoted followers of Newcastle United.

In the short space of 10 years, we had seen our side hang one game away from relegation to the Third Division, and escape it, then stand 12 points clear at the top of the Premier League, and lose it. We had watched the club beat Manchester United 5-0 in the Premier League, and lose to Southend 4-0 in the Second Division. Our heroes had beaten Barcelona in the European Champions League, and lost to Tranmere in the Zenith Data Systems Cup. And we had remained fiercely loyal, as our team has beaten all challengers to reach the FA Cup Final, and lost it. Twice. In successive seasons.

We were talking about being a supporter. Through all of Newcastle United's ups and downs, we had been there. Growing up. Changing. Having our lives, our attitudes, our jobs, our relationships, shaped by the club we loved. Through it all we had remained hopelessly optimistic, defiantly witty, and endlessly devoted to the Toon.

Someone should write a book about being a Newcastle supporter, we decided. Our passion and our obsession. Try to explain why we are as we are.

But how could one supporter hope to represent the opinions of hundreds of thousands of fans? I thought Sir Bobby Robson was the greatest manager ever to set foot in St James' Park. The bloke who stood next to me in a pub in the previous week thought Sir Bobby Robson was a senile old git. I thought Laurent Robert was a wayward genius. The bloke who sat behind me at the match thought Laurent Robert was a... well you get the idea. There are as many different opinions at any gathering of Toon fans as there are black and white shirts. An accurate account of being a Newcastle supporter would need to encompass a representative cross section of fans.

So how to gather the thoughts and opinions of the Toon Army? Stand outside St James' with a clipboard? No, it would interfere with the pre-match pint. So what about that new-fangled Internet? Sounded good. So, a website was designed, press coverage was obtained, contributions began to filter in, and this book began to take shape.

The bulk of the contributions received were responses to the Toon Army survey. You'll find the often eye-opening results discussed throughout this book. I also received hundreds of anecdotes, honest and true, many funny, some staggering, several heartbreaking. A lot of them are featured here, along with the names of the contributors. Some of the names have been changed to protect the drunk and disorderly.

But still, inevitably, these views have been filtered through the mind of one supporter, namely me. Over the season, and over the course of writing this book, my support for Newcastle United has stirred within me every conceivable emotion, from delight to despair and all stops in-between. This is part and parcel of being a football supporter, so if these emotions have at times affected my judgement then I make absolutely no apology whatsoever.

This is the story of the Toon Army in season 2002-03. It's about football. It's about being a supporter. Newcastle United Football Club means so much to so many. This book is about them and for them.

CHAPTER ONE

The Close Season

YOU RARELY see fog on the Tyne these days. It might have something to do with global warming, I don't know. Now Newcastle's Quayside is the glittering social hub of a city of culture. In the shadow of the magnificent Tyne Bridge and its Millennium eye, shipbuilding and heavy industry have made way for trendy bars and million-pound flats. Uphill, along the epic swathe of old Grey Street, the city centre is presided over by Grey's Monument, overlooking the big businesses and famous shopping. All is housed within the confines of the city's protectorate medieval walls.

And looming over the city skyline, overseeing the buzzing bars and sought-after housing, surveying the shopping areas and business districts, and nestled among the medieval ruins of the old castle, is St James' Park.

Newcastle is a football city. Football is our religion, and black and white blood courses through our veins as surely as the Tyne cuts its steady way under our famous bridges. St James' is our magnificent cathedral, the biggest and best city centre football stadium in the country. This is where we worship.

It was summer 2002. A few hardy souls milled about the stadium entrance. The directors' car parking spaces were empty and the club steward, in his Newcastle United jacket, had nothing to do. A couple of kids left the club shop wearing the new blue and grey away shirt. One had 'VIANA 45' on his back. Hugo Viana was the highly rated 19-year-old Portuguese midfielder purchased during the summer break for £8.5 million. He would line up in the squad alongside the club's other big summer signing, 20-year-old £4.5 million defender Titus Bramble. Still we looked for transfer news.

On Northumberland Street, outside Fenwick's store, an *Evening Chronicle* seller shouted 'Ronny Gill!' at shoppers hurrying up and down the pedestrian boulevard. The billboard on his stand offered a tantalising snippet of information: 'TOON IN WORLD CUP STAR TALKS'. Every day over the summer his billboard displayed a similar headline, in the hope of selling a local paper to a football city at a time when there is no football to write about.

In pubs, in schools, in workplaces across the city, the Toon Army turned the wheels of the transfer rumour mill. The friend of a workmate stencilled 'RIVALDO DRIVES PATTERSON FORD' on to the side of a Ford Focus. The brother of a drinking pal saw Rio Ferdinand leaving St James' Park. Sir Bobby Robson mentioned 'the biggest signing in North East history' in an interview during a TV cricket broadcast.

Even the haziest of transfer rumours sets in motion a chain of startling events. A new signing? The heart begins to quicken. The biggest signing in North East footballing history? The hairs on the back of the neck stand up. If we sign him we'll finish higher than we did last season? Sweat appears on the brow. Names begin to be thrown around. Rivaldo? Ronaldo? Possibly, although they are attackers, and Bobby knows we need to shore up the defence to finish higher than we did last season. It's more likely to be a defender. Nesta? Ferdinand? Yes, Rio Ferdinand. He may look like Jar Jar Binks out of the Star Wars movies, but he's one heck of a player. And he's up for sale. And he's a big mate with United's Kieron Dyer. And Bobby raved about him during the World Cup. It could be Rio Ferdinand. Although doesn't he want to sign for Man United? Maybe it is Rivaldo. This is how our minds work.

Me, I hate the summer. It's all sunshine and lollipops and girls with short skirts. I long for a bit of rain and 11 men trying to kick a bit of dead cow between two sticks. June and July constitute my footballing cold turkey, and I get desperate for a fix. I score snippets of information from that ever-spinning rumour mill, and I devour anything that regurgitates the season just gone or anticipates the season to come.

The World Cup provided a minor distraction in 2002, but I didn't really care how well England did in Japan and Korea, just so long as Newcastle's Kieron Dyer didn't get injured.

Following England simply cannot compete with supporting your club side. The national side's passive ranks may be temporarily swelled beyond its regular bunch of Burberry-clad Little Englanders during the course of a big tournament. The country may be whipped into a nonsensical frenzy akin to that which accompanies a Royal funeral. But there is no real emotional attachment. Indeed, the results of the Toon Army survey carried out for this book revealed that a resounding 90 per cent of Newcastle United fans would rather see Newcastle win the FA Cup than see England win the World Cup.

So the majority of the Toon Army watched the world's biggest sporting event in something of a detached state. Seconds after Brazil striker Ronaldinho's killer goal dropped over David Seaman's head, a Newcastle United season ticket dropped through my letterbox. That was my World Cup highlight. I carefully snipped out the label containing my seat number from the accompanying letter and pushed it into its shiny white plastic holder bearing the words 'NEWCASTLE UNITED SEASON 2002-03'.

Now I would wait out the summer. Because when there is no football there is only real life.

Alan from Whitley Bay works at the massive DSS Civil Service complex in Longbenton, where he daydreams about football for 'roughly two thirds of any day'. On the day the local papers broke their run of speculative transfer stories to print the 2002-03 fixture list, Alan spent the morning photocopying and laminating it for the lads in his office. Then someone suggested he should reduce it to a size that would fit into a wallet. Duly, he spent the afternoon reducing, photocopying, and laminating fixture lists for the lads in his office. Taking occasional coffee breaks, of course.

For Alan, the DSS is 'kind of a huge stationery store with a coffee machine'. And, like him, the majority of the several thousand employees on this site spend a lot more of their working day thinking and talking about Newcastle United than doing any actual work. There are, of course, a number of Sunderland fans, or Mackems, working at the complex. But they tend only to show their colours when Sunderland are doing well. As Alan points out, 'They're a very quiet lot'.

The only dress code that applies to non-management staff at the DSS is 'No Football Shirts'. Presumably, this is to avoid all-out workplace war breaking out. There are, apparently, no rules against football screensavers, mousemats, stickers, banners, pictures of monkeys with some abusive comments relating to Sunderland's simian-faced manager Peter Reid, or club crest ties, all of which litter the buildings. I also worked at the DSS for several years, and was disappointed to be once asked to take down a poster showing former Newcastle star Faustino Asprilla dressed as Santa Claus. To be fair, it was six months past Christmas.

At the Nissan plant in Washington, Mackem territory but home to many Newcastle fans, hostilities take a brief respite over the summer. Here, the rivalry between the two sets of fans is felt most keenly. Sean from Washington works shifts with Sunderland fans, and says, 'The scumbags would rather see us beaten than enjoy seeing Sunderland win.' But, in the summer, enmity is restricted to gentle ribbing, and the workers look forward to putting one over on their colleagues in the new season. And, of course, to their summer holidays.

In the summer, black and white shirts travel across the globe. Geordies have the uncanny ability to make a pair of home and away Toon shirts last 14 days. As a result, in bars throughout the world, from Manhattan to Magaluf to Melbourne, you'll find Geordie accents in black and white shirts, making friends, ordering Brown Ale, and singing a familiar song: 'Drink, drink, wherever we may be! We are the drunk and disorderly!'

Summer also provides a window of opportunity in which football supporters can get married. Outside of summer, weddings create a potential minefield for the football fan, particularly when, like myself, you reach your late twenties and your friends begin to form a queue at the altar as if the vicar was giving away free cake. Inevitably, the wedding will invade football's sacred Saturday, leaving the football fan holding a wedding invitation in one hand and a season ticket in the other. The choice is between offending a close friend or deserting your team. And that ain't no choice at all.

In 1998, Tony from Ponteland's wedding clashed with Newcastle United's first appearance in the FA Cup Final for 24 years. Realising 'only the wife and the vicar would turn up', Tony rescheduled. No doubt incurring considerable expense. But it didn't have to be that way. The football season only runs from August through to May. June and July are fine. Excluding testimonial matches and pre-season friendlies, of course.

I became a member of the Toon Army in 1987. I was 13 years old, a relative latecomer, I suppose. Until then, on a Saturday, we'd kick a football about and listen to the matches on a pocket radio. You had to be close to hear it, so whoever was in goal would relay the commentary to the rest of us.

'Waddle's gone close,' the keeper would say.

'Ahhh,' we would moan.

'Keegan's scored!'

'Geddin!'

We played football every chance we got, on the windswept fields on a hill overlooking the Tyne. Of course there were jumpers for goalposts, and the last one there went in goal. Whatever the weather, all day, every day, usually until it got so dark we could no longer see the ball, we'd be there. Games lasted until everyone got sick, or until whoever's ball it was had to go home for his tea. Numbers didn't matter. We'd play 20-a-side or just cup doubles. And if somebody's older brother turned up he could join in so long as he didn't have his big work boots on.

We never had referees. Except for the time one of the lads made red and yellow cards from the back of a cornflakes packet. Any borderline decision was awarded quickly and effectively to the first person to grab the ball, or, failing that, to the winner of a quick punch-up.

And we took it seriously. Every dog walker was a potential scout. No tackle was shirked. One afternoon, Clarkie dislocated his knee. Someone ran to fetch his Mam, and she arrived just as he was being stretchered into the ambulance. 'Hey, lad,' she called out, 'I hope you've got clean underpants on.'

Around that time, my Mam bought me my first Newcastle United shirt, from the old ladies in the little wooden supporter's club shop on Newcastle's now-demolished Prudhoe Place. That old shirt is still my favourite. Manufactured by Umbro from shiny polyester, it featured the broadest of black and white stripes, an 1980s re-imagining of the club badge with the letters NUF underscored by a rotated letter C, and the Newcastle Breweries blue star with the silhouette of the Tyne Bridge.

That was the shirt I wore on that cold winter's day, underneath my snorkel parka, with a scarf bearing the classic 1970s club crest wrapped tightly around my neck, as I made my first visit to St James' Park, alongside my uncle. By now, two of my heroes from afar, Kevin Keegan and Chris Waddle, had gone. I'd watched the Tyne Tees news with a mixture of awe and despair as Keegan had left in a helicopter. Now, as I prepared to see the team in the flesh, the only star player left was Peter Beardsley. But what a player.

That afternoon, Beardsley scored as the Toon beat Aston Villa 2-1. I've been obsessed with Newcastle United ever since.

Within a few months of my first trip to St James' Park, I'd made the transition from 'fan' to 'supporter'. My second match was a 2-1 win over Manchester United, courtesy of a Paul Goddard strike and a Glenn Roeder header. Roeder was club captain and, in the days before the import of foreign players, his 'Roeder shuffle' was about as near to showboating as 1980s football got. As a birthday treat, we sat in the relative luxury of the old West Stand, and stamped our feet and sang as the terraces swayed beneath us. The war whoops of the East Stand's 'Indian Caller' made me laugh so hard I nearly sicked up my half-time Bovril. I was new to all this, but when United scored, when the crowd erupted, we celebrated as one. I was family and I belonged. Newcastle United had a hold of me, and it has never let go.

Within a couple of weeks, I was going to the matches with my mates, up to St James', past the Scottish and Newcastle breweries, with the smell of Brown Ale hanging in the air. We would queue at the juvenile entrance, pay our couple of quid, and stand on the Gallowgate End, under the Scoreboard. You were either 'Scoreboard' or 'Corner', and each section would volley songs back and forward:

'Sing in the Corner!'

'Why's the Corner full of shit?'

My introduction to terrace wit, I suppose.

We preferred the Scoreboard to the even more rambunctious Corner. Anyway, the queues were shorter. And we did have a great time on the terraces. We had to make our own entertainment, because the football was mostly terrible.

From the singing, to the swaying, to the smell of booze and cigarettes in the air, terrace life was infectious, despite the inevitable cold, the surges against concrete stanchions, and various piss-heads relieving themselves where they stood instead of braving the foul-smelling brick wall that was the Gallowgate End toilet.

When Newcastle attacked, the crowd surged, thrusting us forward. And when Newcastle scored, the crowd erupted, throwing our delirious bodies from one direction to another amid a deafening roar.

'GEDDIN!'

'Mr Chips' danced on the electronic scoreboard, and dozens of toilet rolls were flung forward, unfurling on to the pitch. We took to smuggling rolls into the match inside our jackets, an unnecessary precaution back then, at a time when you were allowed into the ground with virtually anything that wouldn't put an opposition player's eye out.

Every member of the Toon Army has their own tale of losing their NUFC virginity. Andy Robson from South Shields' first match was Newcastle 0 Stoke 0 in 1972: 'I can remember being there as if it was yesterday, sitting on my Dad's shoulders in the Gallowgate End, no seats, no roof, packed in like sardines. The atmosphere was so thick it left a taste in your mouth and made your head spin.'

George Stainsby from Newcastle joined the Toon Army in 1979. 'John Lennon was still alive, which was good. *Shoot* was the only real chance of seeing Newcastle United on the telly, which was bad. And my dad took me to the match for the first time. I was seven. My granny had knitted me the world's biggest black and white scarf, and my Dad took me to St.James Park for the game against Wrexham. The feeling of walking up the steps to take our seats in the East Stand was amazing. The pitch edged into my view. I couldn't believe the sight before me. There were proper goals! With nets on! And the smell. The smell of the match. I loved it. It was only when I started going to pubs that I realised the most romantic smell of my childhood was the smell of tabs and stale beer. Newcastle won 1-0 through an Alan Shoulder penalty. At half-time I had a Coke and a Wagon Wheel. My dad had a pint of Exhibition. I needed a wee for just about the entire second half. We nearly lost. We weren't very good. It was the best thing ever.'

Anth Nicholson from North Shields first experienced a match 'standing on a stool tied to the fence, next to my Dad. Twenty years later I took my own son, aged just six months.'

Like most Geordie kids, Anth's son didn't have a choice. Unlike kids in other parts of the country who can choose their side based on the current league standings or the colour of a strip, Geordie kids, by and large, support Newcastle United. The odd child slips through the net and requests a David Beckham number seven Man United shirt. Most are swiftly chastised, then placated with an Alan Shearer number nine.

'From the first match my Dad took me to see I knew I was hooked,' says Jimmy Gibbons from Westerhope. 'The whole thing grabbed me and I knew, no matter what I did in the future, this was where my loyalty would lie. I recently took my six-year-old son to his first match at St James' and I looked at his face and realised what my Dad must have seen when he took me. The magic of being part of this club and its supporters cuts into you and grips your very soul. Newcastle United has shown me highs and lows, excitement and disappointment, love and hate. I would not swap a single minute of it. My son has it all to come and I will be with him for part of the ride. Together, father and son and the Toon. It doesn't get any better than that.'

91 per cent of fans questioned in the Toon Army survey support Newcastle United because of family ties or locality. A lowly one per cent support the club because of recent success. Possibly because that success has been lamentably thin on the ground. Only eight per cent of respondents support Newcastle for any other reason.

'The team represents Geordie pride,' says Davy Patton from Newcastle. 'St James' is the church of the Geordie Nation.'

F. Arthur is an exiled Geordie living in Hartlepool. 'The Toon represents the region,' he says. 'They represent working together and support for one another. All this comes from our history of mining and shipbuilding, industries which played a huge part in social reform. It's also about showing the rest of England we are not a forgotten corner.'

'The club is the heart of a thriving city,' says Anth Nicholson from North Shields, 'a city we defended against the Saxons, the Vikings, and the Tory government. United in black and white we stand.'

Chris Lynch is exiled in Nottingham, but, through Newcastle United, he feels he still has a bond with the city. 'Every away game I go to is like going home, and when you're there you belong. It fills me with pride to be part of the Toon Army.'

Joe from Hexham says, 'Becoming a Newcastle supporter is like joining a secret society, with its own uniform and songs, and something that people on the outside can never properly understand.'

And once you're in, there ain't no getting out. It's a bit like a black and white version of the Mafia, 'this thing of ours', and you can never really sever your ties.

CHAPTER TWO

The Pre-Season

NEWCASTLE United Football Club formed in 1892, when local sides East End and West End joined forces. Since then, the club has won the League championship four times, although never in the last 75 years, won the FA Cup six times, although never in the last 50 years, and won the European Fairs Cup once, over 30 years ago. Still, despite the relative lack of rewards, we love our club to death.

Football has shaped our city and our lives. It is no fluke that Newcastle's startling 1990s regeneration from insular industrial conurbation to buzzing cultural centre coincided with the resurrection of the football club from Second Division minnows to Premiership heavyweights. Now people do bring coal to Newcastle. But, despite the huge changes within the city, the people of Newcastle have remained much the same, being famously friendly, witty, and smart.

We are Geordies, so-called because Newcastle stood loyal to King George during the Jacobite rebellion in 1745. That is one theory, at least. Others link the origin of the name to the Geordie guinea – a coin bearing the face of King George, or to the Geordie miners' lamp invented by George 'Geordie' Stephenson. It is said that a true Geordie must be born within sight of the River Tyne. But people from across Tyneside have adopted the famous moniker. We are proud to be Geordies, united by a love for a city and a football club.

'We are the Geordies, the Geordie boot boys, and we are mental, and we are mad! We are the loyal-est football supporters the world has ever had!'

It was the first week of August 2002, in the run up to season 2002-03. So far this pre-season the first team squad had played six friendly matches, winning five, losing one, scoring 25 goals, and conceding just three.

Hopes were particularly high for the season ahead given the quality of the squad Sir Bobby Robson had assembled. The mighty Alan Shearer led the team from the front. The 32-year-old club captain and quintessential English centre-forward was unparalleled on the pitch or in the eyes of the Toon Army. Welsh international captain Gary Speed, also 32, bossed the midfield. Strong in the tackle, good in the air, and a fine reader of the game, Speedo was something of an unsung hero in the United ranks. Save for these two comparative veterans, the remainder of the first team were all under 30 years old.

Shay Given, the Republic of Ireland goalkeeper, found himself one of the most experienced players in the squad at just 26. Peruvian right-winger Nolberto 'Nobby' Solano and French left-winger Laurent Robert also brought experience to the side. But, excitingly, the vast majority of the first team squad were under 25.

Up front, fiery Welshman Craig Bellamy was the 'Little' to Shearer's 'Large' in a frighteningly dangerous partnership. Quick as a wink, perhaps only the exceptionally talented and energy-filled England international midfielder Kieron Dyer could match Bellamy for pace. Sir Bobby wasn't sure which of the two was quickest, and he refused to allow them to have a race in case it ended in a fight.

In defence, barrel-chested new signing and England under-21 star Titus

Bramble was partnered by Republic of Ireland centre back Andy O'Brien. Andy Griffin, possibly on the verge of an England call-up, and Northern Ireland's Aaron Hughes, a fine servant to the club capable of playing across the back four and in midfield, took the full-back positions.

In addition to this 'first eleven', a number of fine players looked set to push for first team places over the course of the season. Nineteen-year-old midfielders Jermaine 'JJ' Jenas and Hugo Viana looked most likely to break through, with young strikers Shola Ameobi, Lomana Tresor Lua Lua, and Michael Chopra also in the reckoning, and Steve Caldwell and Olivier Bernard ready to cover in defence.

Tonight, at St James' Park, a friendly against Barcelona would provide the first real test for United's class of 2002. And Barcelona and the Toon Army went way back.

The first time Newcastle met Barca, in September 1997, and in the UEFA Champions League – the biggest club competition in the world, United turned the Spaniards over, world superstars Rivaldo, Figo, Luis Enrique, Nadal and all. A 3-2 Champions League victory came courtesy of a classic Faustino Asprilla hat-trick, and, as a worldwide television audience looked on, Newcastle United established themselves as a force in world football for the first time since they won the European Fairs Cup, the club's last notable piece of silverware, way back in 1969.

That fantastic victory over Barca was voted the second-best Toon-supporting moment of all time in the Toon Army survey. Spugsy from Newcastle voted for it, saying, 'I don't mind admitting I was in tears when Tino scored the third.'

Davy Patton from Newcastle didn't vote for it, because he wasn't there. 'I missed the Barcelona match to accompany my girlfriend to an Oasis gig,' he fumes. 'Never again!'

Topping the poll, and the Toon Army's best Toon-supporting moment of all time, was promotion to the Premier League in 1993. Twenty-one per cent of fans voted for Kevin Keegan and company's total domination of the First Division. On the last day of that season, with Newcastle already divisional champions, visitors Leicester City applauded the Newcastle players on to the pitch and local folk rock legends Lindisfarne played a greatest hits set on a temporary stage over the Leazes End. Then Andy Cole and David Kelly both scored hat-tricks, and Rob Lee netted another, in a stunning 7-1 victory. Newcastle's Bigg Market was flooded with delirious fans, climbing lampposts, crawling along window ledges, and singing at the top of their voices:

'Andy Cole! Andy Cole! Andy, Andy Cole! He gets the ball, he scores a goal! Andy, Andy Cole!'

'David Kelly! David Kelly! David, David Kelly! He scored a hat-trick on the telly! David, David Kelly!'

'Robert Lee, Robert Lee, running down the pitch! Robert Lee, Robert Lee, jumps another ditch! Scores another goal, just like Andy Cole! Robert Lee, Robert Lee, Robert Lee!'

'We blacked our faces up with boot polish in honour of Andy Cole,' says Paul Atkinson from Low Fell. 'That would be frowned upon now, I suppose. We also danced on the bonnet of a police car. No one minded. Everyone was on a high. Except for one landlady who chased us out of her pub with a broomstick.'

The 1996 5-0 victory over Manchester United also scored highly in the poll, with 13 per cent of fans voting it their best moment. That was the day goals from Peacock, Ginola, Ferdinand, Shearer, and Albert humiliated the supposed best team in the country, in front of a worldwide TV audience to boot.

'And wasn't it fantastic?' says Kristofer Flinn from Grantham. 'Everything from Darren Peacock opening the scoring to Albert delivering a mouth-watering chip to wrap things up. (And people said he shouldn't have got rid of his 'tache!) From Cantona getting so frustrated that Sir Les Ferdinand had to lead him off for a 'little chat', to the fan who wobbled over to Kev and started to praise him on his hands and knees. It's games like these that make being a Newcastle fan so unique and special. Lets hope for many more nights like that one in October 1996. It's what wearing the Black and White with pride is all about.'

Elsewhere in the poll, consecutive FA Cup semi-final victories against Sheffield United and Tottenham Hotspur in 1998 and 1999, Rob Lee's goal in the Wembley semi-final against Chelsea in 2000, and David Kelly's club-saving goal in the Second Division survival match against Portsmouth in 1992 (possibly the only goal ever to have a commemorative cassette of radio commentary released in its honour – 'Kellyyyyyyyy!'), all figured highly. Perhaps unsurprisingly, the actual winning of silverware was less well represented. Four per cent of respondents remembered the European Fairs Cup win in 1969 as their best moment. Unfortunately, the Toon Army's collective memory was not long enough to allow any domestic trophy to feature in the poll results.

By the time the Champions League return match against Barcelona came around in November 1997, United, under the dour leadership of Kenny Dalglish, were all but out of the Champions League and their domestic league hopes were up the spout. But the Toon Army travelled to Catalonia, boarding the plane, singing, 'We're all off to sunny Spain, Faus-ti-no Asprilla!' On arrival, we took over the Las Ramblas area of Barcelona, a kind of cosmopolitan version of Newcastle's famous Bigg Market. It was all smiles and sangria. An almighty black and white street party. Singing, dancing, grinning. A square of bars with a fountain in the middle was commandeered. There was the biggest conga I had ever seen. Inevitably, there were people in the fountain. Someone shinned 30-feet up a palm tree. Sombreros were purchased, plastic trumpets were parped, and beers were spilled. And no one cared it was raining like a bastard.

Arriving at the Nou Camp, we pressed our noses against glass cabinets filled with European and domestic trophies, alongside the boots and pictures of luminaries such as Maradona, Ronaldo, and Cruyff, in Barca's fantastic museum. The stadium itself was virtually deserted but for the Toon Army, with home fans staying away in protest at recent bad results. Expectedly huge, but eerily silent, the newly-illuminated floodlights banished the dusk to the Catalonian hills which gave the stadium its backdrop. The three-tiered stands – blue, red and grey – were empty. The plastic seats were cracked and faded, and sections were crudely divided with lengths of tape. Two-thirds of the stadium were uncovered and, as heavy rain began to fall, it seemed a strangely lonely place.

Predictably, the match itself was rubbish. Barca overcame the depleted Toon side (with the hopeless Des Hamilton in the starting eleven, not to mention an aged John Barnes, perennially rubbish Temuri Ketsbaia, and a pre-being-any-good Jon Dahl Tomasson) in easier fashion than the 1-0 final score might suggest. We rallied against the elements and the lacklustre entertainment in a desperate attempt to spark to life the atmosphere, but ultimately it was like trying to light a damp cloth. Only three Newcastle players bothered to acknowledge the huge ever-faithful travelling Toon Army at the final whistle. All that was left was to watch the rain, gliding silently down over the floodlights.

It had cost us the best part of the price of a summer holiday to watch our team lose and to see our Champions League dreams washed away in a river of rainwater. But, for some strange reason known only to those of us with black and white blood, and still not entirely understood, it had all been worth it. That's why so many supporters had already taken money saving steps to ensure they could get to at least one Champions League away match this season. Whether that would be in Madrid, Milan, Munich, or back in Barcelona, we would have to wait and see. In the meantime, Barca were back on our turf, and the lip-smacking could commence.

The severe weather warning was broadcast just as I was leaving for the match. It seemed we would be watching Barcelona under rain clouds once again. By the time I reached the city centre, the streets were streaming with water, and the pub was full of steaming matchgoers.

'It's just spittin on, man,' said Steve. 'The Sunderland match. That was rain.'

We didn't talk about the Sunderland match, but Steve was right. On that night, 25 August 1999, the rain was biblical. It seemed to start the moment the team line-up was announced. Mother Nature, it seemed, was a bigger Alan Shearer fan than then-manager Ruud Gullit. The dread-locked

Dutchman left Shearer and striking partner Duncan Ferguson on the bench in an egotistical move that would prove to be his downfall. Our lowly local rivals beat our heroes 2-1, and Ruud Gullit was sacked, against a surreal backdrop of thick rain cloud and rolling thunder. It was a bizarre, seemingly unreal night, voted by 21 per cent of fans in the survey as their worst ever moment supporting the Toon. If, like Kevin Keegan once said, Newcastle United is a soap opera, then this was the episode when Bobby Ewing wakes up in the shower and it has all been a dream.

In fact, that Sunderland match came out joint-top in that worst Toon supporting moments poll. In equal first place were Newcastle's consecutive FA Cup Final defeats to Arsenal and Manchester United in 1998 and 1999. On both occasions the Toon Army descended upon London Town in huge numbers. We sang, and we drank, and we congregated at Trafalgar Square for a mighty celebration of Geordie pride. And then we headed up Wembley Way, with hope in our hearts and the sun on our backs. And then we lost. And as we travelled back, drained of energy and hoarse of voice, in the subdued silence, the echoes of the weekend's cacophony of noise were still ringing in our ears. But still, deep down, you felt it was better to have been there and lost than to have never been there at all. Those matches, along with the semi-final defeat to Chelsea in 2000, which also featured highly in the poll, were key reasons why the Toon Army shed no tears when the old Wembley was demolished. My personal Wembley record was; played four; lost four; conceded ten; scored one. (God bless you, Rob Lee.)

Also featuring among the worst of the worst was the painful Second Division play-off second leg defeat to Sunderland in 1990. After a goalless draw at Roker Park, Sunderland came to St James' and won 2-0. Sunderland were promoted to the First Division and Newcastle spent the next three seasons languishing in the Second. Nineteen per cent of fans voted it their worst Toon moment, and it gets my vote as certainly the most painful blow ever inflicted by our local rivals. 'Although,' says Mike Swinton from Killingworth, 'it remains the only time Sunderland have ever really got the better of us.'

Also featuring prominently in the poll results were losing the league to Manchester United in 1996, Kevin Keegan's resignation in 1997, the FA Cup Final defeat to Liverpool in 1974, and the FA Cup third round replay defeat to Hereford in 1972. Bad memories all. Steve was definitely right. Tonight it was just spitting on.

The rain slashed across the night sky as the St James' Park floodlights drew us like beacons through the darkness. We arrived with hair slicked to our foreheads and rainwater dripping from our noses. There were queues, as always seems to be the case when individual tickets, rather than season tickets, are involved, cold hands taking time to tear off the admission stub. Then the clank of the turnstile, and you're into the back of the stand, filled with fans brandishing plastic pint pots and mugs of Bovril. (Does anyone ever buy Bovril – essentially watery gravy – outside of a football ground?) The toilets, much improved since the days of the foul-smelling brick wall, are negotiated by way of the football fan's unique six-deep queuing system. Then a frame of light at the top of the steps leading to your seat draws you up and out into the stadium, bright, and abuzz with noise.

Football was first played at St James's Park in 1880. Since then, the stadium has undergone scores of redevelopments. But perhaps the biggest changes have been made in the last 10 years. After a £25 million all-seater redesign in 1992, £40 million double-tiers were added over the Milburn and Leazes stands in 2000, bringing the stadium capacity to almost 52,200. And the end result is magnificent – a towering city centre structure, with none of the flat-packed feel of the carbon-copy out-of-town stadia that populate much of the rest of the Premiership.

Over the last 10 years, like many of the Toon Army, I've held season tickets in several areas of the ground. Before 1992, you didn't need a season ticket. You just turned up five minutes before kick-off and paid at the turnstile. Then Kevin Keegan arrived, and everything changed. I bought a standing season ticket for the Gallowgate End, was swiftly moved to the new Leazes stand as the ground became all-seater, then displaced to the Gods to make way for a 'Sports Club', and then moved nearer to the pitch.

And an after-effect of the redevelopment is that, because of these various moves, and because of the lack of spare seats, none of the group of mates I share a pre-match pint with actually sit next to each other in the stadium. So our football talk has to be done away from the ground, in the city's multitude of watering holes. And *Football Focus*' match previews have nothing on ours.

Each pre-match discussion follows the same pattern: Analyse the last match, speculate on our team line-up, assess the opposition, and predict the score. Usually this prediction will be a double – a combination of the score and the first scorer. This will subsequently be backed by the laying down of cold hard cash at Ladbrokes. I have put doubles on before almost every match I've ever attended. And I haven't won once, although I did once get my stake back when Warren Barton 'Centre Parting' failed to make the starting eleven.

By the time I got into the stadium ahead of the Barca match the rain had eased to a mist, drifting through the stands on to the glowing floodlit pitch. The nets billowed from the goalposts in the breeze. Finding my seat, I reacquainted myself with the lads around me, and we chatted excitedly about the season ahead.

Despite being a friendly match, the atmosphere was still heady enough to raise the hairs on the back of your neck. Tino Asprilla, the Colombian who scored that famous Champions League hat-trick, was presented on the pitch to a fine standing ovation from the four towering walls of support around him.

The few moments before the match are pure theatre. First *Carmen Burana* – the Old Spice tune – floods the stadium. Seats clatter as the crowd rises. In the centre circle, the ball boys fan a giant sponsor's flag. Then a glimpse of activity in the entrance to the player's tunnel. Old Spice gives way to Geordie guitar-twiddler Mark Knopfler's *Local Hero*. And, as the teams enter the arena, there is a phenomenal welcome. The match ball, in the referee's hands, shines luminous. Toon players, arms aloft, respond to their welcome with applause for the crowd. Then a handshake, the toss of a coin, and the sharp, shrill sound of the referee's whistle. Game on.

Tonight, after surviving United's strong opening period, Barcelona, fielding the likes of Luis Enrique, Kluivert, and De Boer, took over. The Spanish side fashioned a succession of pinpoint passing moves, carving Newcastle's defence wide open. New boy Titus Bramble and his Greek central defensive partner Nicos Dabizas were in pieces. The midfield was ineffective, and, up front, main man Alan Shearer barely got a kick. Barcelona took an easy 3-0 victory.

The crack in the pub masked our pre-season worries.

'Ah, it'll aal come good, I'm tellin yous.'

'Wor year.'

(Geordies regularly get stick from other parts of the country over our allegedly incomprehensible accent. This is pure bunkum. Those who make this allegation usually pronounce 'Newcastle' as 'Newca-r-stle'. Geordies can clearly see that there is no 'r' in Newcastle. Our dialect, however, is another matter. We have a whole host of phrases with which to befuddle the outsider. 'Aye' is a favourite, meaning 'yes'. 'Wor' means 'our'. 'Whey aye' means 'why yes' and 'whey nar' means 'why no'. 'Haway' means 'come on' as in 'haway the lads.' 'Haddaway' means 'get away' as in 'haddaway and shite'. 'Yem' means 'home' as in 'I'm gannin yem' and 'toon' means 'town' as in 'I'm gannin to toon.' And, although Newcastle is a city, Newcastle is 'toon'. Newcastle United is 'the Toon'. And we, the supporters, are 'the Toon Army'.)

Maybe it would be 'wor year'. In any case, we were not going to be tearing the betting slips up quite yet (we all had money on Newcastle to win the league, at odds as long as 20-1). It was just a friendly, and we should learn from it.

We talked about real life for a short while, and then it was back to football and our hopes for the season, now just a week away. Last orders were called, we finished our drinks, and I headed home, the streetlights reflecting in the rain-glazed streets.

Like the rest of the Toon Army, I longed for a pain-free season. Of course, that could never happen. It is the way of Newcastle United that nothing can ever be straightforward, and each season inevitably emulates the up and down path of a dizzying roller coaster ride.

'Elation and heartbreak occur on an almost weekly basis,' says James Taylor, a Toon supporter from Mackemland.

'The ups and downs are addictive,' says Chris Lynch from Nottingham.

Supporting the Toon is an addiction, something akin to that of a gambler. Every week you are betting on Newcastle winning, placing at stake not just time and money but your very well-being. When the team win, you're on a high, and everything is right with the world. But when they lose, it hurts like a knife. Yet you keep on betting, because you're looking for that elusive jackpot. And, when it comes, you know it will more than make up for everything you've lost in the past.

Maybe losing wouldn't hurt so much if you didn't get involved so much. But that would be impossible. You wonder why success remains elusively at arm's length. Is United too big a club? Are the supporters too passionate? Is there too much pressure on the players? I dunno. But, sooner or later, the law of averages says Newcastle United must win something...

20 Jul 2002	Friendly	SV Capelle 0 Newcastle United 4
22 Jul 2002	Friendly	De Tubanters Enschede 0 Newcastle United 9
24 Jul 2002	Friendly	GVVV Veenendaal 0 Newcastle United 4
26 Jul 2002	Friendly	UDI 19 Beter Bed 0 Newcastle United 5
31 Jul 2002	Friendly	Nottingham Forest 3 Newcastle United 1
03 Aug 2002	Friendly	Wolverhampton Wanderers 0 Newcastle United 2
07 Aug 2002	Friendly	Newcastle United 0 Barcelona 3

CHAPTER THREE

August

I'M NOT particularly ambitious. When I was a kid I had no idea what I wanted to do with my life, and, if the truth were known, I still don't. My only consistent ambition is to see Newcastle United win something. So the start of a new season is always greeted with heady optimism. Newcastle always start with the same number of league points as Arsenal, Man United, and Liverpool, and are still to be knocked out of any of the cups. Wor year.

Newcastle United's season 2002-03 started three days early courtesy of a UEFA Champions League qualifier first leg match, away to NK Zeljeznicar of Bosnia. Some 160 Newcastle supporters travelled to Sarajevo, finding bullet-ridden homes and derelict buildings, reminders of war alongside the thousands of tombstones that surround the Kosovo stadium.

'It's not the kind of place I'd choose for a holiday,' says Cooky from Washington. 'But they sold beer all the same.'

Back in Newcastle, the majority of the Toon Army, were forced to follow the match on the radio, an excruciatingly nerve-wracking experience at the best of times, and worse when your side is involved in a tie worth an estimated £15 million, with Champions League football the gold-plated prize.

Following the match on the radio is best avoided for the most obvious of reasons – you can't see what's going on. To the listener, every crowd noise is a goal, every foul is a penalty, every set piece is a potential goal scoring opportunity, every opposition player is unmarked, and every injury to your star player is career ending. The spectator, of course, knows the crowd is making noise for the hell of it, the foul is outside the area, the set piece is innocuous, the opposition players are safely shackled, and the injury to your star player is just play-acting. For the spectator, the match holds tension in the right places, and easy breathing in others. For the listener, the match is a full 90 minutes of finger-gnawing hell.

But some radio listeners would not agree that following their team on the wireless puts them at something of a disadvantage when it comes to actually knowing what is going on. And these people blatantly flaunt this misapprehension by telephoning post-match radio phone-ins to comment on games they were not even at. North East commercial radio station Metro FM ran a long-running feature during which they would invite listeners to ring in and vote for the man of the match, despite the fact that said listeners had not actually laid eyes on any of the men or any of the match.

For the Zeljeznicar match, my stereo was tuned to local BBC station Radio Newcastle, because Metro FM is banned in my house. This is partly due to their insipid playlist of teen-pop chunder, but mainly due to the aforementioned rain-sodden Sunderland match, after which Metro, despite being based on the very lip of the River Tyne, parodied the famous World Cup Qualifier commentary from Norwegian Bjorge Lillelien that went, 'Lord Nelson, Lord Beaverbrook, Sir Winston Churchill, Lady Diana, Maggie Thatcher...' Metro announced something along the lines of, 'Tony Blair, Sting, Ant and Dec, can you hear me, we gave your boys one hell of a beating.' 'Mackem FM' has now been removed from the radio presets of any self-respecting member of the Toon Army.

Newcastle won the match against Zeljeznicar 1-0, courtesy of a fine goal from Kieron Dyer. Most of us had to wait until the following day to find out just how fine a goal it was. *Look North* showed Dyer break down the left, exchange passes with Lomana Lua Lua and Alan Shearer, and lift the ball over the advancing goalkeeper. A goalless draw in the second leg at St James' Park in two weeks would see United through.

Saturdays and football go together like roast beef and Yorkshire pudding. It's like this: Wake up nursing a hangover, have a bacon sarnie, watch *Soccer AM*, off to the pub for pre-match banter, go to the match, and then back to the pub for post match celebrations-commiserations. All with the added bonus of knowing that you don't have to get up to go to work the next morning. Saturdays are great. Sundays, on the other hand, are rubbish. They are designed only for churchy people and people who like to queue for hours in jam-packed Ikea stores with the horrible spectre of work on Monday looming over them. Saturdays and football are natural bedfellows and their beautiful partnership shouldn't be tampered with by TV folk.

We had spent Saturdays over the close season twiddling our thumbs awaiting the return of football. Now, on 17 August, the Premiership season was finally under way. So how were we spending the first Saturday of the season? Twiddling our thumbs awaiting the return of football, that's how. Because Newcastle's match with West Ham had been put back to the night of Monday 19th to be televised by Sky TV. Premiership supporters have already got used to Sky pushing back three or four matches a season, but now the advent of pay-per-view has more than doubled that figure. Not that I'm against having more football on TV. After all, if you don't like watching soaps or shows featuring do-it-yourself cooks and gardening vets, there's only football or *The Simpsons* left to watch.

Until the arrival of Sky, the football fan had been poorly served by TV. This was particularly true in the North East, where Tyne Tees television fed the football-hungry Toon Army such rubber bones as *Shoot*, featuring the old-school commentary of Kenneth Wolstenholme, the unimaginatively named *The Tyne Tees Match*, Roger Tames' *The Back Page*, and the really quite awful *Café Sport*.

The BBC's *Match of the Day* was always the high-quality exception in the world of football on TV, but, since the BBC lost the rights to cover

Premiership football (when the public broadcaster decided that our licence fee was better spent on screening adverts for the National Lottery than on showing our National Game), the terrestrial responsibility for covering football has fallen, once again, to ITV. The last time ITV held the rights to screen top-flight football, they offered us shoddy and very occasional live coverage via *The Big Match*. Now, with all live rights at Sky, ITV produce only a highlights show – *The Premiership*.

Having jettisoned such failed initiatives as a teatime start, hi-energy montages, Andy Townsend sitting in a van, and Terry Venables playing Etch-a-Sketch, the show is now vaguely watchable. But it suffers from tiresome predictability and glaring bias. Each edition opens with extended highlights of a Manchester United match. Vacuous analysis of that match ('I can tell you he'll be delighted he scored that goal'- 'I'm betting he'll be gutted he missed that penalty') is followed by extended highlights of an Arsenal game. After several commercial breaks and more cripplingly bad summary, somewhere around midnight, brief highlights of a Newcastle game are shown. Unfortunately, it is rarely the same Newcastle game the Toon Army watched earlier in the day, with the cunning editors managing to make even the most rampant Toon victory appear to be a fluke. ITV have an awful track record when it comes to football. *The Premiership* is the latest in a long line of televisual footballing atrocities.

For live football, you need Sky. Unfortunately, in order to watch all available Premier League games you need to pay for both Sky Sports and Premiership Plus, plus cough up your television licence fee. That amounts to an astronomical amount of cash. Any supporter who says he can't afford a season ticket but stumps up to be an armchair fan is, unfortunately, kidding himself.

So Saturday was spent following the start of season 2002-03 via *Football Focus* and *Radio Five Live*. None of it was really important. The big kick-off was yet to come.

Monday evening was warm and I headed out in black and white shirtsleeves to meet the lads. The replica shirt is a dress code staple in

Newcastle, and not just on match days. And short sleeves are always the order of the day on Tyneside, whatever the weather. A trip to the Bigg Market on any given cold winter's night will quickly confirm that Geordie men wear short sleeves and Geordie women wear short skirts no matter how severe the snowstorm. No snow tonight, but rain clouds were gathering as we made our way to the ground.

Inexplicably, Glenn Roeder, the former Newcastle skipper, had apparently brought his West Ham side to St James' Park looking for a 0-0 draw. This was bonkers. Two things anyone with a passing interest in football knew about the Newcastle United side of 2002: 1. Good going forward. 2. Rubbish at the back. It was never 0-0.

For an hour, West Ham, with 10 men behind the ball, did keep Newcastle out, aside from a perfectly decent Alan Shearer goal ruled out for a non-existent push. Then, Tresor Lomana Lua Lua, the bandy-legged Republic of Congo striker, side-footed the ball past West Ham keeper David James. Sixty minutes of built-up frustration were unleashed in a gigantic roar from the 50,000-strong Toon Army. Lua Lua, Bobby Robson's 'little treasure', performed a double somersault in celebration.

A goal down, West Ham were forced to push forward. Newcastle took advantage. Ten minutes later, new signing Hugo Viana floated in a curling cross from the left. Lua Lua, only in the team in the absence of first choice striker Craig Bellamy, powered a header in off the bar. Only one somersault this time, and a hopeful chorus of 'Um Bongo! Um Bongo! Lua Lua's from the Congo!' failed to take off. But West Ham's floodgates were creaking.

West Ham barely got the chance to restart before Lua Lua used great skill on the edge of the box to slide Nobby Solano through on goal. With just the keeper to beat, the Peruvian winger showed superb awareness to cut the ball back to main man Shearer. The ball was laced into the net – 3-0. The floodgates were open. Four-nil would put the Toon top of the table, albeit after just one game.

Four minutes from time, Shearer skinned his marker on the left wing, pushed to the byline, and cut the ball between the goalkeeper and the goalpost. Solano slid in to finish at the far post. Number four. 'We are top of the league,' echoed around the ground. After the silent summer hiatus, the Toon Army had quickly found its voice. Football was back in Toon.

'Jermaine Jenas is the new Patrick Viera, I'm telling you,' we said of our 19-year-old midfielder, over a post-match beer.

'Viana is class, man.'

'Shhh!' hissed around the pub as Bobby Robson appeared on the big screen TV to give his exuberant post-match interview. Hundreds of pub-goers listened in silence, before returning to their conversations.

'Wor year. Wor year.'

The following week, Sky again intervened, this time putting the away match at Manchester City forward to 12.15 on Saturday afternoon. We spent the night before the game sitting in various Haymarket bars watching the Chelsea v Man United televised match, and arguing over whose strongest Newcastle eleven was better man for man – Kevin Keegan's or Sir Bobby Robson's. Keegan, currently at Man City, was the manager who saved Newcastle from relegation to the Third Division, and took our club to within a whisker of winning the Premier League. Sir Bobby took the club from the bottom to the top of the Premiership and into the Champions League. It was not an easy argument to settle.

We picked up the discussion in the car at 7.30 the next morning as we set off down the A1. There were four of us, as there were for most of our away jaunts, with Lee driving, me in the passenger seat, and Steve and Mally in the back.

Lee recently moved, under duress, from Newcastle to Gateshead. From the windows of his flat he can see both St James' Park and the Stadium of Light. He plans to brick up the latter.

Steve has actually experienced winning a league. He isn't 80 years old – he's a part-time Celtic fan. And his few celebratory drinks in the Irish Centre after a Scottish League victory couldn't compare to what would ensue if Newcastle United won the English League.

Mally sits in the posh seats at St James', and he's really the only one of us who's any good at playing football. Or at least he was until he started drinking with us.

'Pavel was a Geordie, man,' someone offered.

'Aye, but he couldn't catch the ball.'

'Give ower!'

'You couldn't rely on him like you can Given.'

'What aboot Shaka Hislop.'

'Give ower!'

This continued on to the M62, into a service station, at the gents' urinal, in the KFC queue, and back in the car, over the moors, where the blue skies turned to black. The rain fell, the Buzzcocks and The Clash played on the car stereo, and we argued all the way to Manchester.

Kevin Keegan was loved on Tyneside. Here he scored goals, got us promoted, left in a helicopter, came back, saved us from relegation, got us promoted again, beat Manchester United 5-0, built the best Newcastle side most of us have ever seen, and oh-so-nearly brought back the glory days.

Before Keegan took the managerial job at Newcastle, the club were teetering on the very cusp of non-existence. In the run-up to the 1991-92 season, Ossie Ardiles' side were favourites to win the Second Division. But, like the design for the team's awful thin stripe-thick stripe 'barcode' home shirts, and as a result of having virtually no good players, everything sharply went A over T. Having lost league games to the likes of Southend, Brighton, and Oxford, with the greatest disrespect intended to those clubs, Newcastle sat on the very brink of Third Division mediocrity. It is not beyond the realms of possibility to suppose that relegation to the Third Division could have been the beginning of the end for Newcastle United. And it is an absolute certainty that, if United had gone down, the club would not currently be troubling the upper echelons of the Premier League. So a change was made.

I remember sitting at the back of a bus gazing incredulously at the front page of the *Evening Chronicle*, waiting for it to sink in: Keegan was back. And how many neutral observers must have stifled giggles when one of the first things Keegan said was, 'Potentially we're sat on the biggest club in Great Britain'? We knew he was right, but then Keegan and the supporters always understood each other. The bubble perm had gone, replaced by a greying feather cut, but it was the same old Keegan.

Thirteen games later, after David Kelly's great volley against Portsmouth, and Gavin Peacock's chip and an own-goal amid mayhem at Leicester City, United were saved. And that should have been it. Keegan had only signed on for 13 weeks. Job done, he could have walked away. But he didn't. And the following season, with Rob Lee and Andy Cole notable additions to the squad, Newcastle decimated the opposition, including a double over Sunderland, in their total domination of the First Division. They were First Division champions – and Keegan had changed the club forever in his first full season in charge.

Then began the roller coaster ride that has been the Premier League. Despite his saving the club, the 'Keegan season' everyone always remembers is 1995-96 – the season where Newcastle supposedly 'blew it' (in fact Manchester United put together a devastating run, and it was they who won the league rather than Newcastle losing it). So the club won nothing. They also played the best football I had ever seen. I was walking into work on Monday mornings with a smile on my face – unheard of before then or since.

United were 'The Entertainers', and everyone loved them. Every football TV show showed slow-motion montages of Toon goals, dubbed to *That's Entertainment* by The Jam, even though the lyrics were totally inappropriate. Ferdinand, Ginola, and Asprilla lit up our lives. But Newcastle couldn't keep it going, and after defeat at Blackburn (courtesy of two goals famously scored by Geordie Graham Fenton, and less famously set up by Geordie Alan Shearer), we knew it was all but over. Keegan never gave up, and his 'I will love it if we beat them' Sky TV outburst was a typically passionate display from the man, and not, as the media insisted, a sign of him cracking under pressure. He had to wait until the following season to fulfil his wish of beating Man United, with Shearer on board, and that legendary victory, 'the five-nil', was probably the best performance by any Newcastle team in living memory.

And then it was over. Keegan walked. No one really understood why. But he had taken the club from the brink of obscurity to the dizzying heights of the Premier League, and showed us the best football we had ever seen into the bargain. To judge his reign as a failure would be to ignore where we came from and where we ended up.

Now Keegan was hoping to perform the same kind of miracle in Manchester. He had already taken City up into the Premiership, but, by all accounts, Keegan had not been able to bond with their fans like he did with the Toon Army. Of course, that didn't necessarily mean he wouldn't turn us over today.

We eventually found a decent parking space in Manchester after several wrong turns caused by Moss Side's almost complete lack of road signs.

'Ah see they've got the same glaziers doon here as they've got in Sunderland,' said Steve as we walked past street upon street of boarded up houses.

We passed one windowless pub that looked like it had recently been gutted by fire. Nevertheless it remained open, and was packed with City fans. We decided to save our pre-match pint for the ground.

This would be the Toon Army's last trip to Maine Road, as Man City would move to a new stadium for the following season. And the old ground looked tired. Its sky blue paint was cracked and dull. Thousands of home and away supporters sat on uncovered terraces wearing club-supplied clear plastic macs, as the rain poured down.

Our side's victory over West Ham had been built upon a tried and tested 4-4-2 formation – the only strategy that has ever worked for Newcastle United in recent history. So it was with despair that we found Bobby Robson had chosen to go 3-5-2 in order to match City's formation. The previous season's Premiership Champions Arsenal always played 4-4-2, and didn't change to suit any other team. Newcastle had changed to suit lowly Premier League newcomers Manchester City. And it would be our downfall.

From the kick-off, City attacked the wings, pulling United's three defenders from side to side like the wooden players on a foosball table. Only Nicos Dabizas, in the centre of the three, looked like he could cope, throwing himself desperately into tackles and into the path of shots. Newcastle created nothing. The supposed whipping boys tore into our team, being wasteful in several attacks, and being thwarted by Dabizas and goalkeeper Shay Given in others.

When City did eventually break through, five minutes before half-time, Darren Huckerby looked to be offside. Uriah Rennie, the Toon Army's least favourite Premiership referee by some distance, got no help from his linesman and allowed the goal to stand. Rennie, who had already been relegated to the Nationwide League once in his short career, made no secret of his dislike for Newcastle's Alan Shearer, and appeared to believe many thousands of supporters in stadia across the country paid to watch him rather than the two competing teams. Thus he posed and preened, extravagantly signalled his decisions, and gleefully made controversial verdicts in an obvious attempt to remain at the centre of attention. In a televised match such as this there were plenty of opportunities for close-ups. Ladies and gentlemen, welcome to the Uriah Rennie show.

In the run up to half-time, United at least mustered a couple of attacks. Kieron Dyer broke through twice, but appeared to have his boots on the wrong feet. The half ended 1-0. Bobby must change it around during the interval, we agreed. He didn't. The second half dragged to a fade, and the match ended in defeat. In only the second league match of the season a side that would be lucky to finish in the top half of the table had beaten Newcastle United.

We drained away from the stadium only to find that Greater Manchester Police had blocked off our route to the car with a hastily erected fence.

On our previous visit to Maine Road, Manchester's finest had seen fit to keep us locked in the ground for 15 minutes after the match, causing a dangerous crush against the exits. Those 15 minutes allowed City's idiot minority to congregate outside the away end. Cue much 'Are you 'avin' it?'

malarkey from Liam Gallagher-wannabes in Hackett jumpers and Stone Island caps. Few Newcastle fans took the bait, but the City yobs attacked the supporters' coaches anyway, as we slinked past to the safety of our car.

This season we were diverted into a succession of nameless and identical terraced streets. As a result we found ourselves heading in precisely the wrong direction for half an hour. After doubling back we spotted the boarded up pub, gratefully regarding it as something of an oasis, albeit one surrounded by Kappa-wearing skinheads brandishing glass bottles.

At that precise moment, Steve's mobile went off. A familiar-sounding tune spun its tinny way around the packed pub car park, attracting several fearsome glances. It was *Blaydon Races*, the Newcastle United anthem, a tale of an 1862 horse race penned back in the day by local troubadour Geordie Ridley. Steve grabbed into his pocket and stopped the ring tone. The pub patrons returned to their beers. Thankfully they did not appear to be fans of 19th century North East Music Hall. They didn't recognise the tune, and we shuffled on.

Finally we reached the car. Lee put a slightly more modern Toon tune, *Home Newcastle* by Busker, on the CD player. And we headed across the moors, back to what we knew.

On the following Wednesday evening, St James' hosted the Champions League qualifier second leg against Zeljeznicar. After the 1-0 win in the away leg, a draw would put us through. Strangely, despite so much hanging on the result, only 34,000 Toon fans turned up, 18,000 less than had attended the friendly match against Barcelona.

The match was comfortable. Halfway through the first half, Kieron Dyer superbly controlled a lofted volley over the keeper from a tight angle. Ten minutes later, Lua Lua swivelled on the edge of the area and rolled a grass cutter into the corner of the net. In the second half, Hugo Viana, with a cracking left-foot volley, and Alan Shearer, with his customary cap-it-off goal, made it 4-0, 5-0 on aggregate, and Newcastle United were through to the Champions League proper.

In the pub we excitedly arranged our travel plans. The draw would take place on the following day, and all challengers were welcome. But if we could combine the match with a decent city break, that would be especially nice. What price Madrid or Milan?

I sat at my desk watching the Champions League draw live, via the magic of technology, on UEFA.com. The screen showed the 32 team names, the 8 groups, and an old man pulling balls from a row of glass bowls. When a team was picked out, its name flashed on the screen. There was a pause of a few seconds. And the team name appeared in its designated group. Newcastle were in pot four, which meant the Toon would be one of the last eight teams to be drawn. Every selection, no matter how inconsequential, was greeted by sweaty excitement.

FC Basle.

'Ohhh!'

Group B.

'Oooh!'

Finally, Newcastle's time came. United couldn't be drawn in groups that already contained the other competing English clubs, Arsenal, Liverpool, and Manchester United, so were guaranteed to be drawn against one of Real Madrid, Inter Milan, Juventus, Bayern Munich, or Barcelona. Group C seemed to be the favourite. With Real Madrid, Roma, and AEK Athens, it offered three great trips on routes furnished by low-cost airlines. Plus the latter two sides looked very beatable.

'Group C! Group C!' I shouted, having already priced the low-cost flights to Madrid on the EasyJet website.

Suddenly Newcastle United flashed.

'Haway Group C! Not Group H! Not Group H!'

Group E.

'Ohhh!'

It was good, but it wasn't quite right. Still, excitingly, Juventus, Feyenoord, and Dynamo Kiev lay in wait. I quickly began to check for flights. And the telephone began to ring.

'Turin, isn't it?'

'Where's Turin?'

Newcastle had by far the toughest group of any of the English sides. The Italian sports paper *La Gazzetta dello Sport* described the draw as offering 'an easy group for Juve', Feyenoord were the current UEFA cup holders, and the trip to Kiev would be just as difficult as it had been during the Toon's last Champions League adventure, when the team battled to a 2-2 draw. But Feyenoord and Kiev, at least, looked beatable. The top two teams would go through to the next round. If Newcastle could win their home games who knew what might happen?

14 Aug 2002	Champions League	NK Zeljeznicar 0 Newcastle United 1
19 Aug 2002	Premiership	Newcastle United 4 West Ham United 0
24 Aug 2002	Premiership	Manchester City 1 Newcastle United 0
28 Aug 2002	Champions League	Newcastle United 4 NK Zeljeznicar 0

Premiership: 10th out of 20

Champions League: Qualified for 1st Group Stage

CHAPTER FOUR

September

AFTER another weekend without football, the night of Monday, 2 September found the Toon Army at Anfield. Previous Liverpool v Newcastle United matches had been declared the 'matches of the decade'. By everyone except for the Toon Army. 'The 4-3s', as they have become known, were two matches, in the consecutive seasons 1995-96 and 1996-97, in which the 4s belonged to Liverpool, and the 3s belonged to Newcastle. In both games, Newcastle fought back from behind, only for Liverpool to grab a winning goal in the final seconds, the football equivalent of being presented with a cream cake only for a large fist to emerge from within and punch you on the nose. Both games were live on Sky TV, and have been replayed almost continuously ever since.

Newcastle United generally get a pretty decent ride from the media, probably stemming from the oft-used 'Entertainers' tag, and due to the general popularity of Sir Bobby Robson. But that doesn't stop TV from sticking the boot in when the team slips up. A good example is the BBC's obsession with Ronnie Radford of Hereford's 1972 FA Cup 'wondergoal' against Newcastle. The Beeb is famously unable to go 20 seconds into any FA Cup broadcast without showing a replay of the goal in all its flukey mud-splattered glory. And yes, I have timed that.

Tonight's Liverpool v Newcastle match was, inevitably, live on Sky TV. Sky, of course, was salivating at the prospect of another hideous humiliation for the Toon. But it couldn't happen again, could it?

The first half ended 0-0, despite Liverpool's goal-scoring chances running into double figures. United were unable to create anything, and continually gave the ball away, putting an already shaky defence under unbearable pressure. Ten minutes into the second half, perhaps pitying Liverpool's wasteful forward line, Newcastle handed them an unmissable chance. Shay Given threw Nobby Solano a 'hospital ball'. Nobby, surrounded by red shirts, couldn't control the pass. Dietmar Hamman, the perpetually-blinking German who left Newcastle under something of a cloud to join Liverpool, leapt on to the loose ball, pushed past Titus Bramble, and drove the ball into the net.

Midway through the second half, another defensive error compounded the misery. Dabizas climbed all over Liverpool's Sami Hypia at a corner. You see it week in week out, and penalties are rarely given. But it was a foul, and the Toon Army couldn't complain when the referee pointed to the spot. Michael Owen, who had previously missed a hatful of chances, made no mistake with his penalty – 2-0 down.

Traditionally, United would let Liverpool get a third before staging any kind of fight back. But not tonight. With 15 minutes to go, Bobby brought on Craig Bellamy and Laurent Robert, both just recovered from injury, plus Jermaine Jenas. Their influence was immediate. First, Robert drove a long-range shot against the goalpost, with Alan Shearer unlucky not to seize upon the rebound. Then the Frenchman charged down the left wing, cut inside, beat two men, and released Bellamy inside the box. Bellamy rushed to the byline, and cut the ball back for the incoming Gary Speed. Speedo smashed the ball into the net from close range. Game on.

The pressure increased as full-time approached. Two minutes from the end, and Newcastle had a corner on the left. Robert wrapped a golden left boot around the ball, sending a delicious out-swinging cross hurtling toward the penalty spot. There, a towering Alan Shearer arrived at huge speed to ram an unstoppable header into the bottom corner of the net. The travelling

Toon Army exploded. 'Shea-rer! Shea-rer!' Shearer wheeled toward them in delight. And he wasn't finished yet. Again, Robert raced down the wing, zipping in a low cross that Shearer met, but could only direct into the smothering arms of the goalkeeper. So nearly a fitting antidote to all that '4-3' palaver. Nevertheless, we were delighted with 2-2, and this time it was the Liverpool fans trooping away from Anfield, scratching their heads and wondering what exactly had gone wrong.

'Oh the way that Beardsley played...
Keegan came and we were saved...
Guessing how much Gazza weighed...
Those were the days...'

The best five players the Toon Army have ever seen play for Newcastle are, in order of merit, Peter Beardsley, Alan Shearer, Malcolm Macdonald, Kevin Keegan, and Paul Gascoigne. I already knew something of this list because I have debated it countless times in various pubs across the world. Now I know for sure, because of the results of the Toon Army survey.

So, according to the survey results, the very best player the Toon Army have seen in a Newcastle shirt is Peter Beardsley. Half of those questioned named him as the best player they had ever seen in black and white. At Newcastle we like our flair players, but we equally highly regard our battlers – those players who give 100 per cent every time they pull on the shirt, like we would, if only we were given the chance. Peter Beardsley, in his two spells with the club, combined fantastic skill with boundless effort, scoring 119 goals in 320 appearances. In possession of the football, Beardsley's quick feet and sharp mind could carve open any defence with a clever shimmy or a perceptive pass. When possession fell to the opposition, Beardsley would battle and harry, tackling back to regain the ball. He scored numerous fantastic goals, with his marvellous strike against Brighton in the season of 1983-84 in Kevin Keegan's last league match being one of the very best ever scored. But perhaps his greatest gift was his ability to create goals for others. While the likes of Andy Cole for Newcastle, and Gary Lineker for England, were gaining plaudits for their goal scoring, it was Beardsley who was creating, serving up their goals on a platter.

Paul Gascoigne is the most naturally gifted player on the list, being regarded by some as the very best English footballer of all time. He played 92 games for Newcastle, making his debut at the age of 17, and left the Toon Army with many fond memories. The then relatively slim-line Gazza showed superb skill and scored some wondrous goals, with his mazy dribble and 25-yard strike against Chelsea in 1988 lingering particularly long in the memory of those who saw it. But Gascoigne is equally well remembered for his comedy antics. As an apprentice, when not taking fishing lessons from Jack Charlton, Gazza cleaned Kevin Keegan's boots. One day he took them home to show his mates, only to leave Special K's Golas on the Metro. He once booked a series of sunbed sessions for teammate Tony Cunningham, but the black centre-forward had little use for them. After a demoralising 4-0 away defeat to Luton Town, after which Luton's players mouthed off in the press, Gazza orchestrated a stunning response in the return fixture. Showing immaculate skill, he led United to an early 4-0 lead, before proceeding to literally run rings around the Luton team. He indulged in lengthy bouts of keepy-uppy, and coerced teammate Kenny Wharton into sitting on the ball. Pure genius. Unfortunately for the Toon Army, Gazza soon followed the likes of Beardsley and Chris Waddle out of the door, being sold, after just three full seasons in black and white, to Tottenham Hotspur for £2 million. However, for better or for worse, he continued to patronise the kebab shops and bingo parlours of Newcastle, and remains a Geordie legend to this day.

Three of the players on the above list are Geordies. Beardsley, Gascoigne, and Shearer grew up, like the Toon Army did, dreaming of playing for Newcastle United. Unlike the Toon Army, they got their wish. And the other two names on the list, Keegan and Macdonald, became adopted Geordies. Some football fans think Yorkshireman Keegan is a Geordie because of his close association with Newcastle United. And Macdonald, despite enjoying probably the most fruitful period of his career at Arsenal, is now a 'professional Newcastle United supporter', being the pundit of choice for local TV and radio.

So our favourite players are five of our own. Is it that we are blinded by loyalty to these players? Does that explain why talented 'outsiders' such as Faustino Asprilla or David Ginola (they polled just two votes each) failed to make the shortlist? Or is it that it takes a Geordie, or an adopted Geordie, to understand what the supporters want, and to ultimately deliver it? A lot of top players and managers have seen their careers dive-bomb during spells at Newcastle. Maybe they suffered because they weren't born in the city. Or maybe they just weren't up for the job.

The worst players list is a much closer call.

'There have been too many bad players to pick one out,' says Andy Robson from South Shields.

'Too many to mention,' says Craig Tither from Gateshead.

Nevertheless, according to the survey, the worst players the Toon Army have seen in black and white are, in order of crapness, Fumaca, Marcelino, Silvio Maric, Mike Hooper, and, in equal fifth place, Rob MacDonald and Frank Pingel. It's worth noting that this list contains four foreigners (two of whom claim to have only have one name), one ornithologist, and no Geordies. Also polling significant numbers of votes were Billy Askew, Kevin Dillon, Wayne Fereday, Des Hamilton, Glen Keeley, and Paul Kitson.

Jose Antunes Fumaca arrived at Newcastle hailed as Brazil's best uncapped player. Of which sport was never specified. Over the course of supporting Newcastle United, I have seen bad players booed, heckled, pelted with Mars bars, and forced to be substituted. But, until Fumaca arrived, I had never seen a bad player's performance met with unanimous, stadium-wide laughter. Quite literally, Fumaca could not kick a football. He was unable to control it, could not pass it, and spent the bare few minutes of his Newcastle United career hugging the touchline, the ball ricocheting off his shin or knee and into touch. He was truly rubbish, barely able to cast a shadow, with one very senior Newcastle United footballer insisting Fumaca was the very worst player he had ever had the misfortune to train with.

Although by no means the least talented player to pull on a Newcastle shirt, Elena Marcelino makes the worst list on account of being perhaps been the most expensive flop in Newcastle United's history. Signed for £5 million in 1999, on wages of £1 million a year, the Spanish defender played only 19 games for Newcastle over three years, due to a long list of injuries, including perhaps the most irreparable broken finger in the history of modern medicine.

Bird-fancying goalkeeper Mike Hooper had a torrid time between the sticks under Kevin Keegan in the mid-1990s. Signed from Liverpool, he eventually cried off citing depression, signing for Sunderland, before becoming an IT teacher, and then a nightclub bouncer.

Strikers Rob MacDonald and Frank Pingel represent the relegation days of 1988-89, scoring a pathetic one goal each as the team spiralled toward demotion. MacDonald smashed more windows at the Strawberry pub behind the Gallowgate terrace than he did balls into the back of the net. Statisticians may point out that Pingel actually scored two goals in his time at Newcastle. Unfortunately, one was a powerful header into his own net. His only proper goal was in that same match, against Liverpool, a deflection off the back of his head that he knew nothing about.

The sad truth is that Newcastle United have fielded more bad players than opinions it was possible to seek. So no mentions for George Reilly, Billy Whitehurst, Andy Thomas, and all. The sad thing is that all of these players have enjoyed the undeserved support of the Toon Army. Like incontinent puppies, they were rubbish but you couldn't quite bring yourself to hate them.

Ian from Whitley Bay summed things up, answering the question 'Who is the worst player you've ever seen in a Newcastle shirt?' with 'I always support the crap lads because I want them to do well for us. But probably Fumaca.'

The evening sky of the 11th was powder blue and cloudless. I had worked late, and I was tired. I leaned my head on to the inside of the window frame of the bus as it trundled into town. For all its intricacies and complexities, football remains a fantastic release from the daily grind. I met the lads in the pub, downed a revitalising pint or two, and walked up to St James', taking my place under the awakening floodlights for the league match against Leeds United.

Leeds had had a poor start to the season under new manager Terry Venables. But within five minutes they took the lead. Kieron Dyer lost the ball in his own half, Leeds' Harry Kewell escaped down the left, and Mark Viduka tapped in the resulting cross. The Toon Army cried for offside, to no avail. Newcastle fought back, but the final ball was missing. When United did break through, the Leeds keeper, Paul Robinson, produced save after excellent save. Three minutes from time, in perhaps Leeds' third attack of the match, Alan Smith rifled home a loose ball. 'We wuz robbed,' said Steve after the match. Newcastle didn't deserve to lose 2-0, but that fact was scant consolation indeed.

After a trip to London resulted in a desperate 3-0 loss to Chelsea, with Gudjohnsen netting twice, with no little help from Newcastle's defence, and Zola scoring a deflected free-kick, the Champions League campaign kicked off proper at Dynamo Kiev.

Newcastle played Kiev during the Toon's last Champions League campaign in 1998, and the Toon Army became acutely aware of the tragic history of this proud club. In 1942, during the German occupation of the Ukraine, Kiev were forced to play a match against the Nazi state team. They were plainly warned, 'If you win, you die.' They defied the warning. Playing for the honour and pride of their people, Dynamo Kiev outplayed and beat the Nazi team, and were lined up in their football kits on a cliff edge and shot dead. Their story puts the so-called sacrifices of the modern day football fan into some sort of perspective. And it underlines the fact that football is a hell of a lot more than just a game.

On the morning of 18 September, 250 Toon supporters turned up at Newcastle Airport at 4am, and were soon snaking around the departure lounge, queuing for a pre-dawn pint. Then on to Kiev, courtesy of Ukranian Airways.

Stay-at-home fans woke to the realisation that seeing the match on TV would involve some sort of militaristic planning. The match was being screened on the obscure ITN News Channel, located somewhere in TV's nether regions, and available at the time only on digital cable. As pubs and clubs were not officially allowed to install digital cable, the choice of venues was limited. Rumours abounded as to which pubs would surreptitiously show it. My local working men's club diverted the channel from the house next door using a cleverly-rigged length of co-axial.

Covert screenings of Newcastle matches are not uncommon, it seems. Dave from Ashington regularly broadcasts Sky matches to his grateful neighbours, 'using nothing more than a TV signal booster I bought in a DIY shop'. He even occasionally rigs up a video camera, and presents half-time analysis from his sofa.

And Tony from Denton Burn secretly intercepts live football, and, indeed, 'blue movies', from his next-door neighbour using 'a set-top TV aerial covered in aluminium foil'. Occasionally, *Coronation Street* interferes with the pre-match build-up, but Tony says, 'I'm able to restrain myself from knocking on the wall – an action which would, of course, blow my cover.'

After the stirring ceremony of the teams lining up to the strains of the Champions League theme tune, the Kiev match itself was a disappointment, with the 42,000-strong crowd falling some 60,000 short of the attendance on United's last visit. Shatskikh lashed in a rocket of a shot after a quarter of an hour, and, 15 minutes into the second half, Khatskevitch nodded in a parried shot. Our European dream began with a 2-0 defeat.

In the North East, the proverbial hotbed of soccer, it's a given that you support your local team. Geordies support Newcastle. Mackems, taking their name from a Geordie insult relating to the early shipbuilding industry ('Sunderland make 'em, other people take 'em'), support Sunderland. It's in the blood, you don't have a choice, and it's as simple as that.

Geordies are often referred to by Mackems as 'Mags', with Newcastle United famously the black and white Magpies. Sunderland AFC didn't have a proper nickname until February 2000, when the red and whites plumped for 'Black Cats' (a tenuous link to a pair of Napoleonic cannons), a decision on par with their nicking the name of their ground, 'Stadium of Light', from Benfica of Portugal. Sunderland rarely call Newcastle fans 'Geordies', a term they secretly like to keep in reserve to use when describing themselves to people who don't know what a Mackem is.

Anyone who has ever held a stake in a North East derby match (and that only means Newcastle United v Sunderland, and not any game involving Middlesbrough) will confirm that the Tyne-Wear derby is the most hotly-contested in England. Bigger than Man United v Man City. Bigger than Arsenal v Tottenham. Bigger than Liverpool v Everton. Almost as big as Scotland's Old Firm match, but without any of the sectarian undertones.

But how can that be? After all, the clubs aren't even in the same city. Newcastle's St James' Park and Sunderland's Stadium of Light are 12 miles apart, separated by the A19 and connected by the Metro system. (The light railway system was finally connected to Wearside in April 2002, 20 years after disgruntled Sunderland taxpayers first began paying for it.)

Ruud Gullit, during his time in the North East, commented that Newcastle v Sunderland wasn't a proper derby match because, he said, the fans don't live and work together like they do in Milan. It wasn't the only thing he got hopelessly wrong during his reign at Newcastle. The Dutchman lost his only Tyne-Wear derby, and his job, when he underestimated the importance of the match, in a St James' Park monsoon on that fateful August day in 1999.

Newcastle and Sunderland fans do work and live together. Mackems work in Newcastle. Geordies work in Sunderland. And in the 'middle ground' – Gateshead, Durham, and Washington – Geordies and Mackems live next door to each other. But the key to the extent of the rivalry between the two sets of fans lies in the rivalry between the two cities, both with their own unique identities, accents, and outlooks. While Liverpool and Everton fans are separated by football, they are united by city. Newcastle and Sunderland fans have no such common ground.

Geordies see Mackems as jealous that Newcastle as a city has, among other things, an International airport, a national railway station, a cathedral, a major concert venue, a renowned nightlife, a set of famous bridges, *Viz* comic, Brown Ale… while Sunderland has none of these.

Mackems see Geordies as arrogant, particularly since Newcastle United haven't won so much as a *Reader's Digest* prize draw for over 30 years. Despite this lack of success, Newcastle have more supporters, regularly selling-out the 52,000 capacity St James' Park, with Sunderland struggling to fill the Stadium of Light since increasing its capacity to 48,000.

Going into 2002-03, Newcastle had won 10 top-class domestic trophies, compared to Sunderland's eight. And Newcastle had qualified for major European competitions 10 times, including the Champions League twice, and won the Fairs Cup in 1969. Sunderland had qualified only once, for the Cup Winners Cup in 1973, and they were eliminated in the second round.

Mackems hate Geordies. It is popularly believed that Mackems would rather see Newcastle lose than see Sunderland win. Although that may not be the case, Mackems do absolutely, positively, unremittingly, hate Geordies.

Sunderland flags and pin badges proudly bear the initials 'FTM', supposedly meaning 'For The Mackems', but actually standing for 'Fuck The Mags'. Geordie fans have suggested 'FTM' could also stand for 'Free Ticket Mackems', in response to the Wearside club's attempts to fill their ground by offering complimentary tickets to schools, businesses, and care homes across the region. That scheme was rumbled when kids, inevitably, turned up at the Stadium of Light wearing black and white shirts. By way of a riposte, Newcastle fans have taken to wearing pin badges bearing the initials 'SMB' – 'Sad Mackem Bastards'.

Of course, Geordies don't like Mackems. They're our local rivals. We work with them, argue with them, and wind them up. But do we hate them? The fact is that, although Sunderland are our local rivals, our real rivals, in terms of winning things, are Manchester United and Arsenal. And the Mackems hate that.

Even the Toon Army song 'Stand up if you hate Sunderland' had fallen a little out of favour as the season began to take shape. We were challenging for the Premiership title, while they were trying to stave off relegation. Knocking the Mackems does our lads no good at all. Who really gives a rat's ass about Sunderland? For Geordies, Newcastle is the be all and end all. It must be the most painful thing in the world for Sunderland fans to gaze upwards from the lower reaches of the league table and see that we don't give a monkey's (excuse the Peter Reid-related pun) about them. And seeing Newcastle United in the Champions League is surely the bitterest pill for Mackems to swallow. So why take a pause from propelling our team into football's biggest club competition to give our irrelevant neighbours a name check?

The Toon Army survey asked, 'What do you think of Sunderland?' 33 per cent of fans said they hate Sunderland. But the majority, 43 per cent, said they simply laugh at Sunderland. Interestingly, absolutely no respondents admitted to supporting all local teams. So the majority of Geordies don't really hate Mackems. Perhaps our relationship with our neighbours from 10 miles down the road can best be summed up by one of our favourite Mackem-baiting songs: 'Let's All Laugh At Sunderland!'

The early-season plight of monkey-faced manager Peter Reid had kept us laughing. Despite keeping Sunderland in the Premiership, he had met mounting pressure from fans, some of who had chosen to voice their dismay by chucking their season ticket books at his dug out. It was generally regarded that Sunderland's visit to St James' on Saturday 21st could easily be Reid's last match in charge.

After just two minutes of the game, Craig Bellamy knocked the first nail into Reidy's coffin. Kieron Dyer released the Welshman, and Bellamy powered away from the Mackem defence. The crowd rose as one, their grey plastic seats clattering. And, in the vacuum created by 52,000 people simultaneously inhaling a sharp intake of breath, Bellamy side-footed the ball under the goalkeeper. Relief and delight. Five minutes before half-time, the Mackems were heading for the exits. Alan Shearer, his head heavily bandaged following a clash in Kiev, drove in a low free-kick from 25 yards. As he wheeled away, arm aloft, Reid's fate was secured. The match ended 2-0.

'Reidy must stay!' sang the Toon Army, and, of course, 'Peter Reid sells tea bags on the telly!' My view was that Peter Reid seemed to be a decent bloke who was skilled at pulling First Division clubs into the Premiership, but didn't have the ability to take them any further. But it was possible that he had taken the club to the limit of their means, and that another manager would struggle to keep them in the top flight.

We celebrated our victory in Newcastle's bars, rammed with grinning black and whites. A derby victory means a rare weekend where you almost look forward to going back to work, only so that you can rib your rival-supporting colleagues. Lee, Steve, and Mally finished the night limbo dancing and drinking 'champagne lager'. Alcohol-induced blackouts have been blamed for the fact that no further information has been revealed.

European action resumed in midweek, with Feyenoord visiting St James'. After four minutes, Nicos Dabizas, Andy Griffin and Andy O'Brien all contributed mistakes as the ball fell to Pardo, who half-volleyed the ball over the advancing Given. It remained 0-1, although opinion was that this was the best Newcastle had played all season. And the Champions League situation became even bleaker in the days that followed, when UEFA announced a three game ban for Bellamy following an off-the-ball head butt in Kiev.

Newcastle's last game in September, on the 28th, was an away trip to Birmingham City. United played reasonably well, although City offered little resistance. In the 39th minute, Shearer dummied a Laurent Robert pass that ran to Nobby Solano, who drove a low curling shot into the bottom corner of the net. And, a minute from time, lanky local lad Shola Ameobi sealed things, bundling the ball past the keeper. Two-nil it was, and, to the tune of *Hokey Cokey*, 'Oh, Shola Ameobi!' rang out across England's second city.

02 Sep 2002 Premiership	Liverpool 2 Newcastle United 2
11 Sep 2002 Premiership	Newcastle United 0 Leeds United 2
14 Sep 2002 Premiership	Chelsea 3 Newcastle United 0
18 Sep 2002 Champions League	Dynamo Kiev 2 Newcastle United 0
21 Sep 2002 Premiership	Newcastle United 2 Sunderland 0
24 Sep 2002 Champions League	Newcastle United 0 Feyenoord 1
28 Sep 2002 Premiership	Birmingham City 0 Newcastle United 2

Premiership: 10th
Champions League Group E: 4th out of 4

CHAPTER FIVE

October

DESPITE the much-needed win at Birmingham City, there were nerves ahead of the big Champions League test away to Juventus on 1 October. Three thousand supporters headed to Turin to watch the match, have a couple of drinks, and look for the steps the Minis came down in *The Italian Job*.

In northern Italy, near to the French border, and a couple of hours drive west of Milan, Turin is, at first glance, an Italian version of Middlesbrough. The travelling Toon Army found a dreary industrial city, choked with Fiats, but also, as the *Rough Guide* travel book pointed out, 'containing gracious Baroque thoroughfares, opulent palaces, sumptuous churches and splendid collections of antiquities and paintings.' Sounded worth skipping the bars for. Or maybe not.

'We were worried about a proposed alcohol ban,' says Lee Shearer from Newcastle, 'but on arrival on the day before the game we were informed that would not be in place until matchday. So we had the rest of the day and quite a sizeable proportion of the small hours of the next to get pissed. Hurrah!'

'We swiftly proceeded to our prescribed dose of strong European lager in the various street cafes dotted around the hotel. The Italians were a little perplexed by this pale-blue skinned breed of people, wearing short-sleeved shirts, wandering around their fair city demanding beer. The more enlightened among us had swotted up on the local lingo by perusing through an Italian phrasebook, but, by the third round of drinks, this plan had clearly been abandoned for the more simple "Three beers please, mate", which was infinitely more effective. Obviously, the barman's Geordie was better than our Italian.'

The night before the match, several hundred Toon supporters were drinking in a bar when a coach containing some famous faces pulled up outside the hotel opposite. Wasn't that Edgar Davids? And that David Trezugeut? It was the Juventus team coach. The Toon Army poured into the street, singing, 'You're gonna get no sleep!'

'I must admit,' says Lee, 'after hearing tales about how mischievous fans have kept awake our Newcastle and England teams when in foreign climes down the years, it was nice to try and do our part for the lads and keep the bastards awake.'

Minutes later, the bar was closed at the insistence of Juve officials. 'Our plot was foiled,' says Lee. 'The rest of the night was all a bit of an alcohol-induced blur, apart from being challenged to a game of international pool by a 3ft 2in Italian with a pony tail, and meeting two Toon fans in the hotel lobby, one of whom was sporting a very fetching leopard-skin vest, apparently removed from a lady of the night only hours earlier.'

By the day of the match, drink and the heady atmosphere had conspired to produce an air of confidence. The drinks ban was surprisingly easily circumvented, and the black and whites of Newcastle congregated with the black and whites of Juventus outside the Stadio delle Alpi.

'We were accosted by a couple of Juventus fans sporting 'Black and White Fighters' T-shirts, stopping their Fiat (what else?) dead in the street to come over and speak to us,' says Lee. 'A strange Geordie-Italian conversation ensued, the conclusion of which was that black and white is, indeed, a splendid set of colours.'

'The stadium looked fantastic from the car park on the outside. Inside, unfortunately, the facilities were pretty dilapidated – no seat numbers, no refreshments and the toilets were, quite frankly, a disgrace. The atmosphere built up towards kick-off, with the 3,500 or so Toon fans, predictably, making most of the racket, although the Italian 'Black and White Fighters' brigade mustered vocal opposition, along with the obligatory flares and giant flags. The vociferous Toon Army began to raise the noise levels to deafening proportions, and the ground beneath our feet literally began to shake. At one point I genuinely thought the stand was going to come down.'

The game kicked off, and the team gave their all. The best chance of the first half fell to Laurent Robert, but the keeper blocked his shot, and the half ended 0-0. But, halfway through the second half, Nicos Dabizas conceded a free-kick just outside the area. Juve's Allesandro Del Piero stepped up into what the Italians ominously call 'La Zona Del Piero'. He duly dispatched his kick – 1-0 to Juve. But United would not give up.

Taking the game to the Italians, a great Robert cross was headed home by Alan Shearer. He turned to celebrate, but the linesman's flag was raised. Shearer was not offside, but Kieron Dyer was, and was adjudged to be in an 'active' position. The goal was ruled out.

Ten minutes from time, Del Piero made it 2-0 with a deflected shot that ricocheted in off Andy O'Brien. And so it ended. The crying shame was that Newcastle more than matched Juventus, and were ultimately beaten by the individual class of Del Piero. But Juve are among Europe's top three or four sides, and it was no disgrace to be beaten by them.

'To put things into perspective,' says Lee, 'one of the lads received a text message from a Mackem, eulogising about their 7-0 defeat of Cambridge in the Worthington Cup that night. And how we laughed. They'll never learn.'

But, after two defeats, and with no goals scored, we knew qualification to the Champions League second round was going to be very difficult.

On Saturday, Newcastle were back at St James', in domestic action against West Bromwich Albion. The Baggies set out to smother the midfield, and, halfway through the first half, their tactic showed dividends as Igor Balis smashed the ball past Shay Given at the near post. But, on the stroke of half-time, that man Shearer squared things up. Balis knocked a close-range pass-back to rookie goalkeeper Murphy. The Albion keeper had no option but to scoop up the ball to prevent it ending up in his net. But he had picked up a back pass, so an indirect free-kick was awarded, 10 yards from goal. With the entire West Brom team strung out along the goal line, Nobby Solano faked a pass to Shearer. The defenders broke prematurely, and had to turn to retake their positions. As they did so, Solano knocked the ball to Shearer, who clinically drove the ball into a gap vacated by the displaced wall. That was 1-1, and Shearer added a second goal half an hour from time, when a great ball from Gary Speed was superbly nodded back by Solano on to Big Al's right boot – 2-1 and Toon blushes were saved.

During a two-week break for International matches, Sunderland finally sacked Peter Reid. It was clear the club had had a replacement lined up, but nobody, except for a group of successful punters who milked the bookies after an apparent tip-off from the offspring of Mackem chairman Bob Murray, guessed it would be Howard Wilkinson. The dour Yorkshireman was the last English manager to win the league. Unfortunately for Sunderland, that had been over 10 years ago, and his experience had been limited to nominal roles ever since. Sunderland fans reacted with apathy, some even calling for the reinstatement of Peter Reid. Wilkinson and assistant Steve Cotterill were not presented to the fans gathering outside the stadium, and Bob Murray had to be bundled into a car and driven away to avoid disgruntled supporters. Mobile phones and e-mail inboxes were flooded with Sergeant Wilko jokes, as the Black Cats offered us yet another welcome opportunity to laugh at Sunderland.

The season recommenced on the 19th with a trip to Blackburn. It was my turn to drive, so I was up bright and early, scraping ice from the car, driving around to pick up the lads, filling up with petrol, and stocking up with newspapers and snacks. The BBC forecast a fine day across the country, with the inevitable exception of Lancashire. We headed down the A1, turned off at Ripon, and negotiated our way along various A-roads, hangovers subsiding enough for a quick sing-a-long to the various splendid hits of Lindisfarne.

Away matches are brilliant, thrilling, addictive affairs. Due to ticketing restrictions, the Toon Army are mobilised in smaller than usual numbers, and this means the individual supporter has a much bigger role to play. As one fan among maybe only 2,000, the influence of your personal contribution of support is that much greater than it is as one among 52,000 at a home match. Players and supporters have a closer bond at away matches. As a result, away supporters have a more pronounced effect on the outcome of the match. Returning from an away win, the victorious supporter is filled with personal pride. Maybe you haven't made such a vital contribution as, say, Alan Shearer, but returning to Newcastle over the Tyne Bridge clutching three points still makes you feel like a returning hero.

On the morning of an away match, a convoy of cars, minibuses and coaches converge on the A1, loaded with black and white shirts, scarves flapping from windows, horns tooting, and the flicking of occasional V-signs for the benefit of opposition fans. Coaches stop on the hard shoulder so fans can relieve themselves over the roadside shrubbery. Soulless service stations are at once transformed into vibrant, seething masses of black and white. Newspapers and sports radio stations provide previews and team news. Maps are rarely required. Travelling football fans know their way around the country's motorways better than the AA.

'Following Newcastle gives me enormous joy and pride,' says Paul O'Pray from Harrow, 'especially away from home, joining up with the Toon Army, raising the roof with non-stop singing in the many stadiums I have visited during my duty as a Toon Army foot soldier. I wear my Toon top with pride. I firmly believe we are the best fans in the world.'

And away matches are about more than just football. 'Even in the late 1970s and the 1980s, when the football was poor and a draw was seen as a good result, the banter and atmosphere were always brilliant,' says Tadger from Rowlands Gill. 'Hundreds of cars on the road, streaming with black and white scarves. Geordies dancing in the back of furniture vans with the back door open. Taking over pubs by half-twelve. Listening to *Star Turn On 45 Pints* over and over again on away trips. The list goes on and on.'

A summer 2002 survey conducted by Co-op Insurance showed that Newcastle supporters travel further and spend more than any other set of fans in their quest to support the Toon. In season 2001-02, those fans who travelled from Newcastle to every away match clocked up a massive 7,782 miles, excluding wrong turns and diversions. They spent an average of £2,033 on rail tickets, £750 on petrol, or £712 on coach tickets. Add to that around £500 for a season's worth of away match tickets, plus refreshment costs. Is it worth it? You'd better believe it.

'Fans who go to the away matches are the real die-hard supporters,' says John Simpson from Wallsend. 'They can't bear to miss seeing their team week in, week out. This means that they'll happily travel 700 miles and spend £200 to see their team get beat at Southampton.'

The obvious logistical problems of getting to away matches are compounded when long trips are scheduled for midweek. The FA seem to give absolutely no thought to away supporters during the planning of the fixture list.

Having a job means travelling from Newcastle to London for an eight o'clock kick-off on a Wednesday night is extremely difficult. Not having a job means you can't afford to travel from Newcastle to London for an eight o'clock kick-off on a Wednesday night. You can see the bind we're in.

Steve Kennedy from Walker was sacked from his first job after sneaking out of work early to get to Grimsby for an Anglo-Italian preliminary round match. 'I got there late and missed wor goal,' he says. Steve now works in personnel and sacks people for a living.

We arrived in Blackburn for midday, grabbing a seat and a couple of pints in The Golden Cup in time to watch Leeds v Liverpool on TV. The pub was already packed with Toon fans, and we swapped team news and tactics. As we walked to Ewood Park, Mother Nature tried to drive us back with a sky-full of gobstopper-sized hailstones. We soldiered on, clothes wet, but spirits not dampened. Within the first 10 minutes of the match, our hopes were washed away.

Four minutes in, Shay Given flapped a cross into the path of Dwight

Yorke. His goal-bound shot was blocked on the line by the hand of Nicos Dabizas. The Greek was sent off, and David Dunn rattled in the resultant penalty. Four minutes later, following not-untypical defensive confusion, Dunn drove in a second. Despite having Titus Bramble warming up on the touchline, Sir Bobby decided not to shore up the defence, instead shifting Nobby Solano to full-back. Somehow, the Blackburn tide was momentarily halted. Ten minutes before half-time, Alan Shearer was pushed in the box, and duly dispatched the penalty for his 300th top-level goal. A marvellous achievement, and the Blackburn fans joined the Toon Army to give their former player, and our current hero, a standing ovation.

Just after half-time, Shearer again showed his class. Laurent Robert drove across an out-swinging corner that Shearer acrobatically leapt to meet, powering an unstoppable header into the back of the net. 2-2. Then Gary Speed clipped a ball over the defence, and Shearer met it first time to finish, only to be flagged offside. No goal, and another turning point. Blackburn sent the ball back up the pitch and won a dodgy corner. After several deflections, the ball fell to Cramlington-born Martin Taylor, who side-footed home to restore Blackburn's lead. Ten minutes later, the game was over. Given lost former Toon player Keith Gillespie's header, the ball ricocheted off Andy Griffin, and ended up in the back of the net. Newcastle's heads went down, and it was no surprise when Taylor rose highest at a corner to head his second and Blackburn's fifth.

The 5-2 defeat was a microcosm of life as a Newcastle supporter. Good crack on the way down, a knockout blow in the first few minutes, then an improbable comeback, followed by a deflating collapse. All accompanied by the unwavering support of the Toon Army. Any other side would have just lost two or three-nil, instead of dangling the carrot of a comeback in front of their long-suffering fans. But not Newcastle United, no, no, no.

On the plus side, there was the marvellous achievement of Alan Shearer. He cemented his reputation as English football's top marksman with his 300th and 301st strikes. For a Newcastle supporter, there can be no greater sight than that of Alan Shearer, head bowed, arm aloft, wheeling away from goal, the football nestling in the billowing net, the agonised goalkeeper strewn in the goalmouth.

But Shearer provides more than just goals. At Blackburn, when United's backs were against the wall, only Shearer and fellow veteran Gary Speed seemed prepared to roll their sleeves up and do something about it.

Shearer is not a controversial character. But on the pitch he's tough and uncompromising. And this has built him a reputation as a player to be both feared and reviled by opposition fans. But, following Shearer's retirement from international football, the same fans who would boo him in a Toon shirt would regret the fact that he no longer wore an England one. In fact, the only reason opposition fans dislike Alan Shearer is because he is Any Good. Indeed, in the aftermath of his fantastic 300-goal tally, football phone-ins were flooded with praise for the man from fans of other clubs from around the world.

Shearer leads by example, and never gives less than 100 per cent. The great Stuart Hall once described him as leading the line, 'like a cavalier, broadsword drawn.' As well as being a deadly goal scorer, he is the best in the business at holding the ball up, he puts in a wicked cross, and is often Newcastle's best defender. The boy from Gosforth is unparalleled. If only we had 11 Alan Shearers.

On the way home from an away match, in the silence, you hear echoes. You hear them when you close your eyes. Roars of delight, thunders of despair, choruses of terrace anthems. They never properly go away, but they're loudest in the aftermath of the match, ringing around the ears in the darkness on the homeward drive up the A1, like some ghostly AM station forever tuned to the head.

Time was you'd need to wait until you saw the Tyne Bridge to confirm you were home. Now, a 65-foot tall rusty metal sculpture, reviled upon its inception, has become a welcoming sign overlooking the A1. The Angel of the North, wings outstretched, reassuringly welcomes the weary Toon Army home.

The following Wednesday, the team faced the daunting task of having to bounce back once more, to avoid elimination from the Champions League by beating the mighty Juventus. The crowd of 48,370 was the highest Champions League attendance so far at St James' Park, impressive considering the club's decision to heavily increase European ticket prices, and the vibrant atmosphere, with TV cameras surrounding the pitch, helicopters buzzing overhead, and songs from foreign tongues riposting our own, left you in no doubt that this patch of grass in front of us, illuminated in the dark night, was the only place to be.

Save for a few scares, there was only one team in it. And, as Bobby Robson's young players came of age, that team was Newcastle United. Titus Bramble commanded at the back (Sir Bobby: 'If you see him stripped to the waist he's like Mike Tyson. But he doesn't bite like Tyson.'), and Jermaine Jenas bossed in midfield ('Jermaine Jenas is a fit lad. He gets from box to box in 90 minutes.'). And, halfway through the second half, Andy Griffin's driven cross was deflected into the Juve net by the Italian keeper Buffon. The night air was ripped apart by a thunderous Toon Army roar. A moment of luck, perhaps, but luck was something United were long due in this campaign. Newcastle held on for the victory, and our Champions League dream was barely, tantalisingly, still alive.

On Saturday 26th it was normal service resumed, with a league match at home to Charlton. United lined up without the injured Craig Bellamy who was nursing a recurring knee problem. And an early central defensive mix-up put the visitors ahead through Shaun Bartlett. But Newcastle's Champions League hero Andy Griffin still had his scoring boots on. Before half-time, the full-back drove a brilliant 18-yard pile driver across the face of the goal and into the top corner of the net. In the second half, Charlton were picked off by a superb Laurent Robert shot midway through the second half. His rasping low left-foot drive gave the Toon a 2-1 win.

Another make or break Champions League match meant ITV had to reconsider its decision not to screen any of Newcastle United's Champions League matches. Previously the schedules had listed six live games, none of which featured Newcastle, despite there only being four English teams in the competition. A heated barrage of telephone calls and e-mails left the network in no doubt whatsoever as to the fury of the Toon Army. And the Toon's victory against Juve meant ITV schedulers had to eat humble pie. So, on the night of the 29th, ITV decided to turn up as Newcastle attempted to beat Dynamo Kiev, the team that had beaten the Magpies 2-0 away in their first Champions League match of the season.

By half-time the score was still 0-0, and Newcastle had lost both centre-halves to injury. Then the run of bad luck extended. A Kiev throw bounced on the pitch and went straight into touch. The referee inexplicably awarded Kiev another throw, and, with two balls on the pitch, the Ukrainians created a passing move that finished with Shatskikh drilling the ball in off the post. Once again, United peered into the abyss.

But United had been the better team, and, with the Toon Army's support shifting up a gear, the persistence paid off. From a Nobby Solano corner, Gary Speed powered a hurtling diving header straight at the keeper, who fumbled the ball into the net. Then Alan Shearer was held in the box. After protest, the ref gave the penalty. Shearer placed the penalty, took his run up, and was stopped by the picky ref, who ordered that he replace the ball. At the second time of asking, Shearer laid the ball on the spot, stepped back, and blasted the ball past the keeper. Shearer spent the rest of the game expertly shielding the ball and winning a series of throw-ins and free-kicks, to run down the clock. It finished 2-1, and, if Newcastle won at Feyenoord, and if Juve could win at Kiev, we would, amazingly, inexplicably, be through.

01 Oct 2002 Champions League	Juventus 2 Newcastle United 0
05 Oct 2002 Premiership	Newcastle United 2 West Bromwich Albion 1
19 Oct 2002 Premiership	Blackburn Rovers 5 Newcastle United 2
23 Oct 2002 Champions League	Newcastle United 1 Juventus 0
26 Oct 2002 Premiership	Newcastle United 2 Charlton Athletic 1
29 Oct 2002 Champions League	Newcastle United 2 Dynamo Kiev 1

Premiership: 8th
Champions League Group E: 3rd

CHAPTER SIX

November

ACCORDING to research carried out by Tesco in 2002, Geordies eat 1.6 million pies every year. That's in total, not each. And the various eateries around St James' Park sell 68,000 pies every season. That puts Old Trafford's paltry 10,000 pies per season somewhat in the shade, although, certainly according to one Roy Keane, Manchester United do a roaring trade in prawn sandwiches.

The match pie is a real curiosity, a re-heated meat product with unidentifiable contents, sweating fat on to a cheap club crest-adorned napkin. It is seemingly heated in some sort of industrial furnace, being served at a temperature approaching that of the sun, with asbestos lips required to deal with its steaming payload of molten gravy. Yet, even more so than burgers, hot dogs, and sausage rolls, the pie remains the undisputed king of football food.

One Toon fan who certainly knows his way around a pie is 26-stone 'Beefy'. Frequently singled out by the TV cameras at televised matches, Beefy is a regular fixture at Toon games, where he can be seen stripped to the waist, baring his huge NUFC belly tattoo. When watching football on TV, Beefy is likely to consume four or five pies, plus a dozen cans of lager, over the course of one match. Now that's dedication to the cause.

Every week, in stadiums across the country, disinterested teenagers in baseball caps thanklessly dish out substandard food and watery pints in plastic pots to baying throngs of hungry and thirsty fans. Overall, football food is out of sorts with the game's modern image.

In American sport, food and drink are very much part of the experience. At baseball and US football matches, vendors roam the stadiums, selling refreshments to spectators in their seats. And those refreshments include beer. In English football, alcohol is not allowed within view of the pitch, a draconian measure that implies that the modern football fan cannot enjoy a couple of drinks without turning into some sort of raging idiot. Of course there is the possibility of spillage, but better cold beer than hot coffee.

For booze, the majority of fans avoid St James' beakers of beer, and seek pre-match refreshment away from the ground. Newcastle is home to in excess of 100 pubs. And a good deal of them are within stumbling distance of the stadium. While current pubbing hotspot the Quayside, favoured by Toon fans and players alike, may be too far away from St James' for pre-match shenanigans, the Haymarket and the Bigg Market are more than accommodating. From The Strawberry, right in the shadow of the Gallowgate stand, to The Trent House on Leazes Lane, down to The Irish Centre, Rosies, The Newcastle Arms, The Goose, The Three Bulls, The Percy, The Hotspur, Oz, and Old Orleans, all along Percy Street, the Toon Army's tens of thousands of pre-match drinkers are excellently catered for.

And then there is the Bigg Market, the spiritual home of *Viz* comic's Sid the Sexist ('Tyneside's Silver-Tongued Cavalier') and the Fat Slags ('Oh Lordy!'). By night it is swarming with drunken lads in pastel-coloured Ben Sherman button-down shirts, and shivering lasses in low-cut tops and tiny belts of fabric masquerading as skirts. On a match day it is black and white through and through, with the likes of The Blackie Boy and The Old George serving up drinks, and with Idols and The Vault serving up the additional attraction of, shall we say, off-colour entertainment, or 'topless tottie' as it is referred to in the native tongue.

Even discounting Lord Abdul Latif of Harpole's famous Rupali restaurant and its 'Curry Hell' challenge ('finish it and it's free'), there is plenty of good food to be had around the ground, not least the delicious Geordie staple of ham and pease pudding stottie cakes flying out of bakeries and café's on the approach to the ground.

And it is best to stock up on food before you reach the stadium. Inside St James' Park, the Toon Army bemoan the lack of availability of the popular balti pie and the rollover hot dog, both of which made season 2001-02 a memorable one for culinary connoisseurs. Now the average Toon fan can typically be seen, in the moments before a match, clutching only a good old-fashioned non-specified-meat pie, plus a betting slip, both of which have approximately the same nutritional value.

November began with a surprisingly solid defensive display. Another young player, Scotsman Steve Caldwell, came into the heart of the defence for the visit of Middlesbrough. And he marshalled things with aplomb.

Only a small group of people think Newcastle v Middlesbrough is a derby match. Most of them live in Middlesbrough, but a few of them work in a TV studio on Newcastle's City Road. The local ITV station is called Tyne Tees. So imagine their delight when teams from the rivers Tyne and Tees do battle. Cue much hyping of the supposed 'Tyne-Tees derby'. Newcastle v Middlesbrough is not a derby match, and every time Tyne Tees Television bill it as such they are insulting the intelligence of the fans they seek to represent.

Middlesbrough had improved immeasurably under new boss Steve McClaren, and they attacked from the off, but it was Newcastle's Shola Ameobi who rattled in the opener halfway through the first half. Boro continued to press, but the Toon kept them out. And, just before full-time, Caldwell got a deserved goal, volleying home from a corner. Two-nil, and not much more than a workmanlike performance, but no less satisfying for it. 'That was soured by the Smoggies' constant moaning,' said Lee, as we laughed off Boro's complaints that they should have had two penalties. And, as McClaren and company whinged all the way back to Teesside, we happily toasted our three points with a round of cold drinks.

NOVEMBER

Just two days after the Boro game, United returned to St James' to take on Everton in the Worthington Cup. Newcastle had gone straight into the third round of the competition on account of their European involvement. Sir Bobby Robson understandably rested a number of key players, but United's patchwork team looked uncomfortable from the start. Ten minutes in, Kevin Campbell rose unmarked at a corner to head Everton into the lead.

The game trundled along, before exploding into life in the last 15 minutes. First Hugo Viana slid captain-for-the-night Kieron Dyer in on goal. Dyer drove the ball under Everton keeper Richard Wright for an equaliser. Sixty seconds later, Dyer got a fantastic second, turning outside the box and curling a superb 20-yarder into the corner of the net. Two-one, and Newcastle were heading through to the next round. Until, five minutes from time, local lad and former Toon player Steve Watson grabbed an equaliser – 2-2. The match went to extra time.

After 100 minutes of play, another former Toon player, Italian defender Pistone, headed a Dyer cross into his own net. During his time at United, Pistone was given a pig's heart as a Christmas present by squad members who felt he was often lacking that particular organ. Some wags among the Toon Army suggested that it was about time Pistone came good for Newcastle. But, two minutes later, Steve Caldwell handled the ball in the area. He was sent off, and David Unsworth rattled in Everton's penalty. Three-three, and the game headed for penalties.

There was an audible groan from the Toon Army at the final whistle. Over the past 20 or so years, Newcastle United had lost every competitive penalty shoot out they had taken part in. Things looked bright when Toon keeper Steve Harper saved from Unsworth. But young Viana missed, as did teenage debutant Michael Chopra. At least they had the guts to take a penalty, while experienced centre-forward Carl Cort refusedly stood with his coat on. Then Laurent Robert, nursing a broken jaw that would keep him out of action for the next few games, saw his penalty saved by Richard Wright. Everton went through. Newcastle went out. Mickey Mouse cup anyway.

Every time our club slips up, the media delights in reminding us of our lack of silverware. We don't need to be reminded, but supporters of other clubs give us stick every week.

'You've never won fuck all,' sing rival fans. Yes we have – four leagues, six FA Cups, and a European Cup.

'Where were you were you were shit?' Standing on the Gallowgate End alongside thousands of other like-minded souls. Not always enjoying it, but always there.

'Are you Sunderland in disguise?' Clearly not – that would contravene any number of FA rules. And, anyway, we are, literally, in a different league to Sunderland.

And so we respond: 'We are the Geordies. The Geordie Boot Boys. And we are mental. And we are mad. We are the loyalest football supporters the world has ever had.' 'loyalest' isn't even a proper word, but it works so well in context.

'We'll support you ever more.' Through thick and, most usually, through thin. We'd love it if you won something, but if you don't we'll still be there.

'We love you Newcastle we do. We love you Newcastle we do. We love you Newcastle we do. Oh Newcastle we love you.' Haway the lads.

United's trip to Arsenal on the following weekend was dire. Newcastle mustered no shots, and won no corners. With Patrick Viera immense for the home team, the only surprise was that Arsenal only won 1-0, courtesy of Sylvain Wiltord's first half goal. Perhaps United's minds were on the midweek European match – the must-win match in Rotterdam against Feyenoord.

The potential ramifications were many, but what it basically boiled down to was this: To qualify for the Champions League second group stage, Newcastle would need to beat Feyenoord in Holland, and Juventus would need to beat or draw with Dynamo Kiev in the Ukraine. Juventus had already qualified, and were likely to play a scratch eleven, so Toon hopes on that front were not high. Failing that, a draw against Feyenoord would allow Newcastle to filter into the UEFA Cup.

On 13 November, 3,000 Toon fans travelled to Feyenoord's impressive De Kuip stadium, and the team responded to their magnificent support in fine style. As per usual, Shearer to Bellamy looked to be the key. Shearer, so typically, won everything in the air, and Bellamy, playing his first game for three weeks, was on to his flick-ons like a whippet.

On the stroke of half-time, Shearer rose, and Bellamy raced away, rifling the ball past the goalkeeper. One-nil, and, as they say, what a great time to score.

Just minutes after half-time, the lead was doubled. Kieron Dyer worked his way into the box and ignored the waiting strikers to brilliantly pick out Hugo Viana on the edge of the box. Showing great skill, Viana expertly drove a left-foot shot into the far corner of the net. If that wasn't good enough, news filtered through that 'Juventus reserves' were beating Kiev. Champions League second group stage here we come. Of course, this was Newcastle United, and it could not be that simple.

Up to this point, Feyenoord had barely put two passes together, but, suddenly facing a European exit, they began to knuckle down. On 65 minutes, substitute Mariano Bombarda burst on to a through ball and scored. Buoyed, Feyenoord assaulted Shay Given's goal. Crushingly, inevitably, five minutes later they equalised, Anthony Lurling smashing home from the edge of the box – 2-2. We had been so close to Champions League survival, but now we were holding on to a UEFA Cup place by the skin of our teeth. Feyenoord continued to press. If they snatched a winner, Newcastle would finish bottom of the group and fail to qualify for either competition.

And then the final minute. Nicos Dabizas launched a long ball upfield that was expectedly won in the air by Shearer. The captain's flick-on this time found Dyer, who burst into the box. Racing past the defence, Dyer found himself with the keeper to beat. Choosing to place his shot, he rolled the ball to the keeper's left. The goalkeeper went to ground. And saved it. The ball spilled wide, virtually on to the touchline. Then, seemingly from nowhere, came Bellamy. Rifling the ball at pace from an acute angle, the

Welshman drove the ball against the goalkeeper. And into the net. 'YESSSSSSSS!'

The Toon Army went crackers. Virtually the last kick of the game, and we had scored. Truly this was one of the very best moments in Newcastle United's long and proud history.

And it got even better. First the final whistle was greeted with delight. Then, after a few anxious moments, there was confirmation that Juventus had held on for a victory over Kiev. Newcastle were through to the second group stage of the Champions League for the first time in the club's history. United were also the very first club to qualify despite losing their first three matches. The team would take its rightful place among the very best 16 sides in Europe. The club would earn around £10 million as a result of qualification. And we fans could look forward to mouth-watering trips to play Europe's elite.

'This is one of the best moments ever,' said Dave, who I'd experienced innumerable Toon-related disappointments alongside. And it was. It was one of those brilliant pay-off moments that made it all worthwhile. This was why we did this. This made sense of it all. Me, I didn't say anything. Nothing intelligible, anyway. I just jumped up and down, grinning.

The Toon Army also gained a second team that night. Juventus, the grand old lady, had not let us down. We were united in black and white. The Juventus vice-president, Roberto Bettega, said, 'We promised we would help Newcastle United and we did.' Geddin.

The crucial Champions League second group stage draw took place that Friday. There was a much more relaxed atmosphere than that which had accompanied the first round draw. The draw format and the quality of the other participating teams guaranteed that Newcastle would net three juicy opponents. And so it was.

Group A: Inter Milan, Barcelona, Bayer Leverkusen, and Newcastle United.

Within minutes of the draw, cheap flights had been snapped up for Milan and Barcelona. The EasyJet website creaked under the weight of hundreds of bargain-seeking Geordies. Within a couple of hours, the best flights were sold out. A visit to the San Siro, and a return trip to the Nou Camp were simply too much to resist. We would visit Barcelona in December, Leverkusen in February, and Milan in March. Bring them on.

Two minutes into the following Saturday's home league match, Southampton brought us somewhat back down to Earth. James Beattie, hyped by the press as 'the new Shearer', whacked a great shot in off the post from outside the box. But Newcastle rallied. Ameobi knocked in a close range goal just before half-time, and in the second half, Aaron Hughes got on the end of a Viana pass and toe-poked the ball past the goalkeeper. A 2-1 victory. Not a vintage performance, but enough to send the Toon Army home with hats on the side of their heads.

The away trip to Manchester United is one of the least difficult for travelling Toon fans to negotiate by road. Give or take traffic delays, it's possible to make the journey in less than two hours, barely changing gear from the time you touch the A1 to the moment you pull into your parking space. Once you are there, there is the small matter of facing the most consistent side of the last 10 years. Old Trafford has not been a happy hunting ground for the Toon in recent seasons. But perhaps this season could be different.

Manchester United are the Harlem Globetrotters of football – undeniably talented, but arrogant with it. They are at the forefront of the corporate money-mad movement that is ruining football. They're a brand name masquerading as a football team. Football matches are interruptions in their hectic promotional schedule. They have already once taken the disgraceful step of withdrawing the FA Cup. It would be a natural progression for them to withdraw from the other competitions, only surfacing to play exhibition matches and appear in animated form on episodes of *Scooby Doo*.

Merchandise is king at Old Trafford. Dodgy stalls line the routes to the ground, and fans in Man United shirts, hats, coats, and scarves crowd around the Manchester United Superstore, clutching red carrier bags full of officially licensed products. Tourists gleefully take photos and shoot video footage to record their trip to the 'Theatre of Dreams'. (I have a better dream – it involves Sir Alex Ferguson and a red-hot poker.) Newcastle supporters just grab a couple of pints and head into the ground. We did come here for a football match, after all.

The bars around the ground refuse entry to away fans, so drinks are had at a redbrick bar in the middle of an industrial estate some way from the stadium. Then into Old Trafford for a bottle of 'Manchester United Bitter'. We did once gain entry to the nearby Trafford Bar when our mate Kersey, a Manchester United fan with, surprisingly enough, no connection whatsoever to Manchester, had a word with the bouncers. But watching other black and whites being turned away as we sipped bottles of Becks among a bunch of Man United fans left a bad taste in our mouths. And the ill-feeling welled as the pub's clientele sang Sad Geordie Bastard to the tune of *Daydream Believer* without being able to agree on whether to cheer up Kevin Keegan, Alan Shearer, or Bobby Robson.

Manchester United were without Roy Keane, David Beckham, Rio Ferdinand, and Nicky Butt. The newspapers reported this with vigour. Newcastle United were without Laurent Robert, Hugo Viana, Titus Bramble, and Steve Caldwell. The newspapers did not report this at all. But this was still a great opportunity to beat them – if the real Newcastle United turned up.

Unfortunately, from the start, it was obvious that the real Newcastle United would not be in attendance. With Ryan Giggs looking unstoppable, Manchester surged forward. Halfway through the first half they got their reward, through Paul Scholes' clinical shot. But, 10 minutes later, despite failing to muster a single attack, Newcastle drew level. Olivier Bernard's speculative cross-shot looped over keeper Fabien Barthez and into the net. Manchester responded with two carbon-copy goals, both created on Newcastle's wayward right flank, both finished easily by Ruud van Nistelrooy. Three-one down at half-time, and the match seemed to be over. But that was counting without Alan Shearer.

Five minutes into the second half, the Toon skipper cracked home an unstoppable 25-yard free-kick to notch his 100th top-flight goal for the club. Three-two, and Newcastle were back in the game. For a few seconds. Again, Newcastle's right flank was exposed, and van Nistelrooy netted his hat-trick goal – 4-2, and six goals from six shots in the game. This was the killer goal, but then Ole Gunnar Solskjaer compounded the Toon Army's misery by barging Aaron Hughes to the ground, and making it 5-2. Craig Bellamy headed another consolation goal from Shearer's knock on, and, briefly, it looked like Newcastle could actually get something. But Manchester held on, and the game finished 5-3.

We had scored three goals at Old Trafford, and Alan Shearer had notched another remarkable record. But the only consolation to take from the game was the performance of the Toon Army. 'Sixty-thousand Muppets!' we sang at the catatonic home fans. And we were right. If it wasn't for the Toon Army you would have been able to hear the proverbial pin drop. They don't like fans standing up at Old Trafford. The local council had threatened the ground with closure unless fans stopped standing. But the Toon Army stand wherever they go. This season the stewards decided not to push the issue, and it was amusing to see thousands of Geordies standing throughout the game, while any Manchester United fan standing was quickly told to sit down by nearby police officers. But the non-stop support from the fans was not enough to elicit an effective response from the team.

'It's great being part of an elite group of fans who support this team almost without question,' says Dave Stuart from Prestwick. 'But I have often thought in the past that the team doesn't deserve this support. Or rather these supporters deserve much more than they get.'

After the match, trooping away from Old Trafford, I was torn between two thoughts. The first was that I should stop putting my time, money, and sanity on the line in the face of continued abject let-downs. The second was that I must keep putting my time, money, and sanity on the line, because one day things will come beautifully together, and I'm damn sure I'm going to be there when they do. Hope, always hope.

The finger-licking Champions League second group stage kicked off with a home game against the mighty Internazionale of Milan. Inter, with the likes of Christian Vieri and Hernan Crespo, looked formidable. And Toon fears were realised within seconds of the kick-off, when Morfeo netted following a desperate Dabizas lunge. And things got much worse.

In the fifth minute, Craig Bellamy was rabbit punched by Materazzi, and responded with an elbow. The referee had no option but to show a red card to Bellers, although Materazzi escaped punishment. United were a goal down and playing with 10 men against one of the best teams in the world. Just minutes later, Alan Shearer was in the thick of things, raising his arm against Cannavaro to free himself. The ref took no action. Ten minutes before half-time, Almeyda scored a great second. A minute into the second half it was three, with Crespo scoring. Newcastle were actually playing some neat football, and Nobby Solano helped to raise spirits, with the returning Robert putting him in to score a consolation goal. Ten minutes from time, Recoba came off the bench and scored a fantastic goal with his first touch. Much of the Toon Army applauded the strike, despite the fact that it ruled out any Newcastle comeback.

The 4-1 defeat was Newcastle's biggest ever European defeat, outplayed with 10 men, and disappointed the team couldn't have given a proper account with 11. Bobby Robson pointed to the quality of the opposition, saying, 'We weren't playing Cuckoo United, you know.'

In the aftermath of the match, there was much huff and puff in the media regarding Bellamy's sending off. Some fans rang football phone-ins demanding that Bellamy be sold. Former Toon idol-turned-pundit Malcolm Macdonald as good as echoed these criticisms. Few detractors mentioned, despite Bellamy's stupidity against Dynamo Kiev and now Inter Milan, that the club would not be in the 2nd Group Stage of the Champions League had a certain hot-headed Welshman not scored a famous winner in Feyenoord.

NOVEMBER

04 Nov 2002 Premiership	Newcastle United 2 Middlesbrough 0
06 Nov 2002 Worthington Cup	Newcastle United 3 Everton 3(2-3 on penalties)
09 Nov 2002 Premiership	Arsenal 1 Newcastle United 0
13 Nov 2002 Champions League	Feyenoord 2 Newcastle United 3
16 Nov 2002 Premiership	Newcastle United 2 Southampton 1
23 Nov 2002 Premiership	Manchester United 5 Newcastle United 3
27 Nov 2002 Champions League	Newcastle United 1 Inter Milan 4

Premiership: 7th
Worthington Cup: Eliminated
Champions League Group E: 2nd – Qualified for 2nd Group Stage
Champions League Group A: 4th out of 4

CHAPTER SEVEN

December

THE local papers love their 'Superfans'. These are fans who, in the opinion of regional newspaper hacks, go above and beyond the call of duty in supporting their team. One fellow unfortunate enough to have this dubious honour bestowed upon him is 63-year-old Tex Widdrington from Shieldfield. Tex is a United Superfan on account of having painted his Ford Scorpio black and white. According to the *Evening Chronicle*, he is 'Car-Toon Crazy'. He has engraved the names of every Newcastle United player on to the bonnet, and has also painted the hallway of his flat black and white. But he hasn't actually been to a Newcastle United match since 1955.

Is he really a Superfan, or is he just a bit eccentric?

The *Chronicle* is forever bringing us tales of fans who have attended matches while visiting the region from Australia or the USA. They may also have visited the MetroCentre, but does that make them the world's most devoted shoppers?

So who is the real Superfan? The guy who travels to Newcastle from New Zealand in a hot air balloon shaped like a bottle of Brown Ale, wearing an oversized black and white top hat and a hand-painted wooden rosette? Or the guy with the quiet, genuine love for a club that can make his day, or break his heart?

While the papers churn out their tales of fans who have made one-off journeys from Japan or America to watch the Toon, they rarely mention the thousands of fans who regularly travel thousands of miles every season to watch the Toon. Some 23 per cent of respondents in the Toon Army survey were away match regulars, clocking up almost 8,000 miles and spending over £2,000 to travel from Newcastle to away games each and every season. And the survey found the Toon Army as a whole travels an average of 1000 miles and spends an average of £1000 in supporting NUFC over a season.

The survey also revealed the worldwide extent of Newcastle's support, with replies from California, Canada, Pakistan, New Zealand, and many points in-between.

While 50 per cent of respondents described themselves as local Geordies, 33 per cent said they were exiled Geordies.

Mark Hadfield now lives in London, and travels 700 miles to each home game. 'But I love every minute,' he says.

Jon Sutcliffe is from Enfield, and says supporting Newcastle gives him 'a secure identity in a foreign city.'

Dale Imray lived in Whitley Bay before emigrating to New Zealand. Dale and his sons get up at 3.45am to follow the Toon on TV. 'I have to apologise to the teachers if the kids are less than attentive in afternoon lessons,' he says. Before emigrating, Dale took Ryan and Jack to St James' to see the team in the flesh one last time. He also showed them his heritage stone, 'Dale Imray Forever Black 'n' White', paved into the stadium floor. 'I made them promise that when I passed away they would bring the grandkids here, and lay a flower on my stone, and tell them exactly how much Newcastle United meant to their Grandad. They said, 'We promise, Dad,' and I hugged them close as a tear rolled down my cheek and I took a last look at my spiritual home.'

Mike Mullins is exiled in Austria. 'All of my neighbours here are more aware that I'm a Toon fan than that I'm English!' he says. 'It's great that these neighbours will come round to watch games and genuinely support us – a team they had never heard of 10 years ago.'

Closer to home is Colin Stuart. 'As an exile living in Kent and working in London,' he says, 'I am fiercely proud to be a Geordie and a Newcastle United supporter, as is borne out by the way I respond to comments made to me by the mass of London club and Man United 'supporters' I meet. I love Newcastle United. I bleed black and white.'

The official Football Association Fan Of The Year 2002 is also a member of the Toon Army. Pete Osborne from Margate travels 700 miles and six hours for every Newcastle home game. And not a black and white Ford Scorpio in sight.

Newcastle United also has its share of celebrity fans. And, unlike the many London media darlings who have inexplicably pledged their allegiance to Manchester United, most of the Toon Army's famous affiliates are Geordies. Tree-hugging rock star Sting is perhaps the biggest star to support the Toon, but he is apparently too busy saving rainforests and having tantric sex to attend any matches that aren't FA Cup Finals or glamorous European away ties.

Tony Blair claims to support Newcastle, and fondly recalls sitting on the Gallowgate End as a boy. Unfortunately, the Gallowgate End was a standing section until the 1990s. When asked to name the first game he went to, Mr Blair said he couldn't remember. Perhaps that is because, according to Mackem musical lyricist Sir Tim Rice, Blair once actually confessed to him to being a 'Sunderland devotee'. Could Mr Blair's famous Premiership-boosting televised head-tennis match with then Newcastle boss Kevin Keegan have been conducted under false pretences? Not so, says the PM. Apparently his favourite website is the really quite rubbish official NUFC site, although he doesn't visit it during office hours.

Thankfully, some celebrity Toon fans are more dedicated. TV stars Robson Green, Jimmy Nail, and Gabby Logan all actually attend Toon matches. Gabby started supporting Newcastle while studying at Durham University. 'It was the time that Kevin Keegan was setting Newcastle alight,' she said. 'I could just as easily have become a Mackem!' Luckily, the ITV football presenter chose black and white, although she could have been forgiven for having misgivings when she put on a very posh frock and travelled all the way up to Newcastle at the end of the 2001-02 season to present Alan Shearer with his North East Player Of The Year award, only to find that the event was being held in the back room of a brewery.

Ant McPartlin and Declan Donnelly, 'TV's Ant and Dec', are the celebs most regularly spotted at Toon matches. The pair regularly attend home and away matches, and often mention Newcastle United on their TV shows. And, despite their fame and money, the pair still long to pull on black and white shirts, with Ant saying, 'If I could click my fingers and swap everything I've got now to play for Newcastle, I would.'

Everton are a team with good support and a proud history. But, in recent years, they have flattered to deceive. Like the Toon Army, Everton fans deserve more than they get. But, with new manager David 'Moe out of The Simpsons' Moyles at the helm, and with the much-hyped junior pie-master Wayne Rooney up front, the Toffees' form in the run-up to their visit to St James' had been good.

So, the Toon Army were pleasantly surprised to see United launch attack upon attack on the Everton defence, apparently determined to hand out a battering. And, when key Everton defender Joseph Yobo was sent off for pulling back Craig Bellamy, three points appeared to be in the bag. But, totally against the run of play, a long ball out of Everton's defence found Kevin Campbell, who barged through the middle, and pushed his shot between Shay Given's legs – 0-1. Newcastle continued to assault the Everton goal, without being able to find the final ball to beat keeper Richard Wright. The clock ticked down, and the crowd began to believe it might be 'one of those days'. As time ran out, and with Everton still holding on, hundreds of Toon fans headed for the exits. More fool them.

With four minutes left, Laurent Robert launched a long ball up to Shola Ameobi. Shola beat David Unsworth for the ball and headed it into the path of Alan Shearer. Thirty yards from goal, Shearer hit a ferocious dipping volley that rocketed over the helpless Everton keeper into the goal – a brilliant strike of the kind few other footballers in the world could score. Even the big man himself later admitted it was the best of his career. And there was more to come. Craig Bellamy darted down the left, and cut in a wicked byline cross which Everton's Li Tie could only deflect off his keeper into the net. Bellamy half-heartedly took the applause, perhaps realising he was still in the Toon Army's doghouse after his sending off against Inter. And the final whistle blew. A deserved, but last-gasp win.

The only people who can be excused for leaving a match early are those souls who are informed over the tannoy: 'Can Mr X please make your way to the Maternity ward. Your wife is having a baby.' Cue one grinning bloke hurrying down the steps to the cheers of the fans around him. Those who leave a match early for any other reason, maybe to be first out of the car park, or to catch an early bus, haven't properly understood the principle behind being a football supporter.

Clearly there is a distinction between 'fan' and 'supporter'. You can be a 'fan' of a pop group or a television programme. It's a one-sided affair. You enjoy the music or the show, end of story. Being a 'supporter' is more complex. There is give and take from both sides. It's a two-way thing. You enjoy the match, sure. But in return you offer backing, appreciation, and funding. The *Oxford English Dictionary* defines the verb 'support' as: '1. keep from falling or sinking… bear the weight of. 2. give strength to, enable to last or continue.' That is the role of the supporter. Professional football couldn't exist without us. And you can't offer support from an armchair.

You have to be there and be involved to properly enjoy the spoils of victory. If you're already standing on the Metro platform by the time the final whistle blows, then the victory belongs not to you but to the fans who stayed to the end and propelled their team toward the three points. The victory belongs to the supporters.

A trip to freezing cold Aston Villa on the following weekend saw plenty of chances created for each side. But only Alan Shearer, with an 82nd minute header from an Andy Griffin cross, found the net. Shearer celebrated in front of the travelling Toon Army, and three points, from only United's second away win of the season, were in the bag.

Fate regularly throws curve balls at the Toon Army, but the bizarre events on our return to Barcelona, for United's Champions League match on 10 December, were pulled from the very bottom of a particularly nasty bag of tricks. In a throwback to our last visit, the team would be without their first-choice strikers, with both Bellamy and now Shearer, following UEFA's intervention, banned after their indiscretions against Inter.

Nevertheless, 4,500 fans headed to Catalonia, only to be greeted by torrential rain. Apparently, the last time Barcelona had such severe rain was five years previously – on the very night of our last Champions League visit. Once every five years, and we catch it twice. Apparently, the rain in Spain falls mainly on the Toon Army.

The Toon Army travelled by plane, boat and train, at great expense, and just a fortnight before Christmas, to support the team. Some travelled on tours organised by the club or by independent travel companies. Others, like my own band of reprobates, made their own way to Barca. And our journey was a disaster from the start.

Our bargain basement travel itinerary involved a cheap train from Newcastle to King's Cross, and a cheap EasyJet flight from Luton to Barcelona, plus various train and taxi transfers along the way.

Arriving at Newcastle's Central Station at 7am, we found our train had been severely delayed due to a power failure. Forty-five minutes later, despite having non-transferable tickets, we decided to jump on to another train. We arrived in Kings Cross two hours late, and legged it past the capital's army of beggars to the Thameslink station to catch a train to Luton. Boarding the train, one of the lads was almost decapitated by the slamming metal doors (with no Metro-style 'Stand clear of the doors please' warning like we're used to in Newcastle).

We arrived at Luton Airport just in time to catch our flight. And there were more than a few eyebrows raised when a female voice came over the aeroplane's PA and said, 'This is your captain speaking.' Of course, there is no good reason why a woman shouldn't be able to fly a plane. But the only female pilot any of us could think of (apart from plucky air stewardess Karen Black in *Airport 75*) was Amelia Earhart. And she ended up crashing into the Pacific. But it wasn't our pilot's fault that the plane was hit by lightning, although the teeth-shattering landing wasn't particularly pleasant.

Luckily the plane didn't have to be reverse parked, so we arrived promptly in Barcelona at 5pm. Within minutes we were on our way via taxi to our hotel, which the driver had some trouble finding because the company we'd booked it through had given us the wrong address. At this point the rain was little more than a drizzle.

After dumping our bags, we sought out refreshments and a taxi, and headed to the ground. By now, a storm had broken. The taxi sloshed through the streaming streets with windscreen wipers working overtime. Lightning flashed ominously in the distance.

By the time we reached the ground, the rain was torrential. We took cover in a bus shelter with a bunch of Barca fans. Thunder boomed overhead, and explosions of lightning lit up the sky. Commentators often refer to the atmosphere surrounding football matches as 'electric', but this most literal of interpretations was beyond a joke.

Then, two hours before kick-off, a Spaniard with a radio turned to us, said 'Football', and made an 'X' with his arms.

The match was obviously off, but, as the rain eased, we decided to walk around to the away entrance to see what the crack was from the Toon Army. And we were amazed to see hundreds of fans heading into the ground.

'Is the match on?' we asked a steward.

'Yes, yes,' he said, ushering us through the entrance.

We headed into the stadium and found around 1,500 similarly duped fans. An announcement over the tannoy confirmed the match was off, but told us to stay in the stadium until 'our busses' were brought around. We tried to explain to a policeman that we hadn't come in a bus, but he just waved a big stick at us. So, we were locked in the ground for around an hour. We went out to have a look at the pitch, and there was no question that it was unplayable. The stadium was even emptier than it had been in 1997, and the small bunch of us sang 'Shit ground, no fans' as the rain, predictably, began to ease off.

By the time we were released from the stadium, still an hour from kick-off time, the rain had completely stopped. General consensus was that if Barca had kept the pitch covered during the week's rainstorms, something which even English non-league teams seem to be able to do in the run up to big televised games, then the pitch would have been perfect.

Outside, a sizeable gang of Barca toughs shouted abuse as we left the stadium. One Toon fan had his flag stolen, but one of our lads managed to pull him away before things escalated. After walking for half a mile with no sign of an empty taxi, we jumped on a bus and, somehow, ended up in Las Ramblas. The square of bars with the fountain in the middle that was swarming with black and whites on our last visit was completely deserted, with a pile of plastic pint pots indicating that it had been livelier pre-match. So we found a decent bar full of Toon fans, and had a great night, with pint-suppage running into the early hours.

The crack from the Toon Army was typically brilliant, despite the circumstances. It soon emerged that the match had been rearranged for the following night, when most of us would be back in Newcastle. We heard numerous stories, varying from those who had been sitting in the bar all evening after being told the match was off as early as teatime, to some who had already managed to book new flights via mobile phones, to others who would be in the air on the way home while the rearranged match was being played with no means of knowing what was going on. One fan we met, from the London Supporter's Club, had £120 plus his match ticket stolen, and then had to travel home alone to go to work while all of his mates stayed in Barca.

Full marks were due to the thousands of Toon fans who managed to extend their stay to see the match. For us, like probably 2,000 others, money and work commitments meant it was impossible. We waited at the EasyJet check-in desk until the very last moment, desperately trying to think of a solution. But it wasn't to be. So we trooped home, heads shaking all the way in disbelief. The return journey was trouble-free, save having to tell a parasitic pair of Sky Sports journalists feverishly awaiting our arrival at Luton Airport to stick their camera where the sun don't shine. We were back in the Toon an hour before kick-off, just in time to watch the match on the telly.

Meanwhile, back in Barca, the remaining members of the Toon spent a day in the sunshine, and headed to the Nou Camp to find the pitch in perfect condition. Claire Brissenden, an exiled Geordie from Chesham, was among the bunch who had managed to stay.

'Those who had stayed were determined to create enough noise to make up for those who were now watching the game back home,' she says.

The crack was great. 'We're supposed to be at home', and, 'Stand up if you've missed you're flight', were among the evening's repertoire.

Unfortunately, the team's effort didn't match that of the fans. Within the opening 10 minutes, Barcelona had scored, with the inexperienced Lua Lua giving the ball away on the edge of his own area, only for Dani to sweep in a fine goal. But, 15 minutes later, the scores were level. Solano bustled his way to the edge of the box and found Kieron Dyer, who laid the ball to Shola Ameobi. The immensely impressive young Geordie coolly slotted home – 1-1. Could this be the greatest night in Newcastle's history? Er, no. Andy Griffin was skinned for the umpteenth time by Marc Overmars, and the unmarked Patrick Kluivert scored – 2-1 to Barcelona at half-time.

In the second half, despite Newcastle playing some good stuff, Barca increased their lead. An innocuous corner caught out Shay Given, Motta headed goalward, and Dyer, shamefully asleep on the post, with one arm resting 'I'm-a-little-teapot'-style on his hip, failed to clear. The game ended in a 3-1 defeat. Not the most famous of matches, but the events surrounding it will live long in the memories of the Toon Army.

'Friendships were made in Barcelona,' says Claire, 'born of a shared passion for a club that tempts you with the prospect of European football, takes you to the edge of your seat, and keeps you coming back for more. Milan here we come...'

Just three days later, Newcastle United's globetrotting supporters made the relatively short 668-mile round trip to Southampton – in fact the longest journey in the Premiership. Still, despite hardly having time to catch a breath, there were enough Newcastle fans at St Mary's Stadium to contribute to Southampton's biggest-ever Premiership crowd.

Southampton manager Gordon Strachan later described the match as classic. Perhaps the well-travelled Toon Army were too bleary-eyed to fully appreciate it, as it seemed like average fare to most black and white eyes. Nevertheless, the support was magnificent. Craig Bellamy responded shortly into the second half. Beating two men, he curled a shot from the edge of the box that nestled in the far corner of the net. It was probably his best goal for United. But, perhaps predictably, Southampton immediately pushed upfield, and Chris Marsden scored from close range. A number of decent chances followed, but the game finished as a draw.

In the space of eight days, less than two weeks before Christmas and despite all of the expense that entails, the Toon Army had travelled in numbers to Aston Villa, Barcelona, and Southampton, providing second-to-none support at each.

A home game against Fulham, and Newcastle's last match before Christmas, was a relaxed affair after the tribulations of the previous week. The black and white Santa, a regular fixture at festive games, seemed to be absent, but the season of goodwill was nevertheless under way.

Within the first 10 minutes former Toon player Alain Goma had gifted United a goal. The French defender, seemingly flustered by the boos of the Toon Army, panicked in possession and played a crazy back-pass to his goalkeeper Edwin Van Der Sar. Under pressure from Bellamy, Van Der Sar knocked his clearance right at the feet of Nobby Solano. With the keeper only a couple of yards off his line, Solano placed a perfect lob into the net.

Fulham created little, but it was not until midway into the second half that the game was killed off. Dyer played in Bellamy, who drove a left-foot shot across the keeper. Alan Shearer could even afford a penalty miss, his eighth failed spot kick for Newcastle, blasted very high and wide into the Gallowgate End.

So the Toon Army got three points for Christmas, as well as a whole host of Newcastle United–related merchandise of varying quality and use. On Christmas morning, Newcastle's pubs and clubs were full of happy punters proudly wearing their brand new Newcastle United sweatshirts, and showing off Toon watches and jewellery. There were, of course, those who had to grin and bear low-quality Newcastle United gifts. Seemingly, some people will buy anything with 'Newcastle United' on it. My Mam bought me a ballpoint pen with a picture of cavorting dolphins on the side and the words 'Newcastle United' stamped over the top.

'What's this?' I asked, rather ungratefully.

'It's Newcastle United,' she explained, matter-of-factly, as if dolphins and Newcastle United Football Club were natural bedfellows.

At least it showed more imagination than the staple football fan Christmas gift – the 'hilarious' Nick Hancock-type footballing gaff video. Ho-ho, there's Ian Wright, and he's pulling a funny face! And there's that goalkeeper throwing the ball into his own net! And look – it's Rene Higuita doing his scorpion kick! Again! For the love of God, football fans are intelligent people. Enough with the footballing gaff videos.

But even high-quality football gifts can disappoint. A fan who sits near Mally told him he'd received an official Newcastle United sweatshirt from his wife. He took one look at it and threw it in the bin, proclaiming, 'I divvent wear a jumper to gan to the match!' He proudly told this story while shivering in a short-sleeved Toon strip, with those around him all toasty in winter coats and hats. Once presents, family niceties, and the increasingly unfunny *Only Fools And Horses* specials have been negotiated, Christmas means only one thing to the Toon Army: Football.

Boxing Day. A bank holiday. A traditional day of relaxation. Unless you happen to be travelling down to Bolton for a one o'clock kick-off. The Premiership clash with Wanderers meant an 8.30am start and, for our driver Lee at least, an early night on Christmas Day. Considering this was a Boxing Day match, there was surprisingly little seasonal cheer in Lancashire. We arrived early at Bolton's flat-packed out-of-town Reebok Stadium, and headed straight for the pub. Only to find a line of burly bouncers blocking our entrance.

'Sorry lads, you'll not get served in here,' one bouncer said.

'Why's that?' we asked.

'Because when Sunderland came down here last season they tore the place apart.'

'So what's that got to do with us?'

'Well, yous are all the same up there, aren't yous?'

Of course, this was the very worst reason this meathead could possibly have given. Much furious ranting to the effect that in that case Bolton fans must be the same as Man United fans fell on deaf ears.

'There's a bar on the other end of the ground that'll serve you,' he lied.

The same thing had happened on our last visit to Bolton. The Tesco store next door to the ground also refused to sell alcohol to Newcastle fans, despite that chain gleefully letting Geordies rack up record-breaking booze sales at its Newcastle store.

The annoying thing is that away fans can get into any bar they like in Newcastle, where away shirts are often seen mingling with black and whites, and there is very rarely any trouble. Do we need to implement some sort of 'tit-for-tat' system where the fans of clubs whose surrounding bars ban away fans are similarly excluded on their visit to Newcastle? Some away destinations are great for a pre-match pint, but the increasing majority have at least some bars that exclude away fans. If this is the decision of the bar owner there is little we can do about it. But if, as certain bouncers insist, it's a police decision, then it's an infringement of civil liberty that we can certainly do without.

Inside the Reebok – a vacuous tin shed, almost indistinguishable from the likes of the Stadium of Light and the Riverside Stadium – a horrific line-up of podgy pre-teen cheerleaders in skimpy skirts performed a gormless dance routine. When the match got under way, Bolton's goals were greeted by a burst of James Brown's *I Feel Good*, accompanied by fully-grown men running the length of the pitch with oversized Bolton flags.

'If this is the future of football, I don't want to be part of it,' said Lee, as the game we loved imploded around us.

Yes, 'Bolton's goals'. There were, infuriatingly and pathetically, four of them. First, Jay Jay Okocha fired in from the edge of the box. Shearer equalised, sliding the ball under the keeper after good work from Solano and Dyer. But, within a minute, Bolton restored their lead. Given failed to line up his defensive wall, and Ricardo Gardner fired in a free-kick. Then, on the stroke of half-time, Michael Ricketts isolated full-back Griffin, and scored an easy header.

A poor Speed pass gave Ricketts a second and Bolton a fourth halfway through the second half. With Bellamy asking not to play, it was his stand-in Ameobi who grabbed Newcastle's second, his shot deflecting in off Dyer. Then, with 12 minutes still to play, Shearer rifled in a superb 20-yard free-kick – his 350th goal – 4-3 down, but Bolton were terrible. Surely Newcastle could go on to get a draw.

Substitute Lua Lua ran for goal and was tripped on the edge of the area. Enter our old pal, referee Uriah Rennie. First, the worst referee in the Premiership booked Lua Lua for diving. Then he delighted in booking his nemesis, Shearer, for doing his duty as a captain and politely questioning the decision.

Newcastle didn't come back, and lost 4-3. United's record under Rennie was now; played 13, lost 8, drawn 3, won 2. For a side that had regularly troubled the top of the Premiership, that imbalance could not be ignored.

We trooped home to our turkey sandwiches, consoling ourselves with the fact that we could possibly be spared a trip to Bolton in the following season by Wanderers' relegation. Memories of flag-wavers and men dressed up as lions made the defeat even harder to forget. What a shame you no longer have to put your occupation on your passport. 'Football Ground Flag-Waver'. Have these people no dignity? The day's other league results were kind to us, and we gnashed our teeth at the missed opportunity.

Tottenham Hotspur were improving under Glenn Hoddle. But the former

England manager's pre-match comments on his visit to St James' that Spurs would replace Newcastle among the Premiership elite were as brainless as his bonkers and little-questioned belief that disabled people are paying for the sins of a previous life. Within 20 minutes, Gary Speed had rammed Hoddle's words down his throat, with Robert's long throw flicked on by O'Brien, and Speed's right foot driving the ball home.

But United's midfield was soon decimated, with Speed, Dyer, and Solano all leaving the pitch with injuries. Speed's hernia problem looked to keep him sidelined for some time. He would be a huge loss, with Bobby Robson commenting, 'We can't replace Gary Speed. Where can you get an experienced player like him with a left foot and a head?'

Nevertheless, in the second half, another quick Robert throw found Bellamy, and his chip to the back post was headed home by Shearer. Nicos Dabizas frayed nerves with a spectacular diving header into his own net, but second-class Spurs never looked like scoring without such assistance. Our old favourite and former star striker Les Ferdinand was afforded a thrilling standing ovation when he appeared as substitute, only to be comically booed, in typical Toon tradition, upon his first touch.

The match finished 2-1, and Newcastle ended the year placed fourth in the Premiership, and still in the Champions League, with the FA Cup to come in January.

01 Dec 2002 Premiership	Newcastle United 2 Everton 1
07 Dec 2002 Premiership	Aston Villa 0 Newcastle United 1
11 Dec 2002 Champions League	Barcelona 3 Newcastle United 1
14 Dec 2002 Premiership	Southampton 1 Newcastle United 1
21 Dec 2002 Premiership	Newcastle United 2 Fulham 0
26 Dec 2002 Premiership	Bolton Wanderers 4 Newcastle United 3
29 Dec 2002 Premiership	Newcastle United 2 Tottenham Hotspur 1

Premiership: 4th
Champions League Group A: 4th

CHAPTER EIGHT

January

THE new year of 2003 began for us on Newcastle's Quayside, attempting to watch Sir Bobby Robson set off the city's fantastic firework display. But several thousand people blocked our view, and we were unable to negotiate them without fear of dropping our commemorative New Year kebabs. So, we retreated to the pub, and instead saw Bobby later on that day, at his rightful place in the NUFC dugout.

A 7.45 kick-off on a bank holiday meant hangovers and a lack of public transport had to be overcome. Liverpool were the visitors, and their strangely negative brand of football promised a dull start to 2003. Sore throats rallied to provide support. Moaning big-nose Phil Thompson was dispatched to his seat with a rousing chant of 'Sit down Pinocchio', and old-school terrace chants like 'The Corner!' were given a welcome airing. The St James' Park crowd of 52,147 was almost 9,000 bigger than the attendance at the Anfield reverse fixture earlier in the season. Newcastle completely bossed the match, but only Laurent Robert's deflected free-kick found the net, giving Newcastle a 1-0 win.

Robert's goal ended a turbulent week for the Frenchman. The winger should have been one of the stars of the Premiership in his second season in English football. But, for one reason or another, he had failed to find form.

As a result, he had become a target for the St James' Park boo-boys. To be fair, Robert had been no worse than fellow winger Nolberto Solano over the course of the season. But his work rate was questionable, and a series of largely mistranslated press articles in which he was accused of criticising club and colleagues didn't help.

Thankfully, the boo-boys among the Toon Army rarely actually boo. And rightly so. If you want to boo, you should go to a pantomime. There had been a few occasions of booing at the final whistle after poor performances over the past couple of seasons. But this season the disgruntled minority had limited their grumblings to annoyed grunts along the lines of, 'Robert, man! You're shite!' and, 'Get that French bastard off, Robson!'

Many of those same boo-boys had, not so very long ago, criticised Alan Shearer, insisting that he was finished. During Ruud Gullit's reign many Newcastle fans agreed with the Dutchman's decision to drop Shearer for that fateful, rain-lashed Sunderland game. Many wanted Shearer to walk. If he had, and if Gullit had stayed, where would the club be now? At that time it was actually possible to hear, on occasions, the words 'Shearer' and 'shite' in the same sentence. To utter those words in season 2002-03 would amount to Toon Army Treason. Now, week in, week out 'Shea-rer! Shea-rer!' rings around St James' Park. All players have bad runs, and jumping on their backs doesn't help them through it.

Obviously it is only a minority of football fans who think that abusing their team makes them play any better. The majority know that the booing of your own team actually gives the opposition a boost. The problem is that, often, the supportive majority can't seem to find the voice to drown out the dissenting minority.

Robert, as the current scapegoat, had also fallen foul of the media. After the Spurs match, he stormed into the St James' Park pressroom and confronted *Evening Chronicle* journalist Alan Oliver. Apparently a punch was thrown, and a cup of tea was sent flying, before Kieron Dyer and Lomana Lua Lua managed to pull the Frenchman away. The incident followed an alleged 'witch hunt' perpetrated by Oliver against Robert in an attempt to drive him from Newcastle. The reporter denied he wanted anything other than for Robert to do well for Newcastle, and refused to make a big deal out of the incident.

Traditionally, the first weekend in January means the FA Cup third round. The round where the big boys enter the ring. The giantkilling round. So, the BBC dusted off its footage of bloody Ronnie Radford, and Newcastle headed to Wolverhampton to take on First Division Wanderers.

The Toon Army were strangely subdued, and not just because of coins and spittle raining down upon them. United provided little for their fans to cheer. After six minutes, Wolves opened the scoring, with Paul Ince driving low past Shay Given. Within half an hour it was two-nil, with an unmarked Mark Kennedy scoring easily. United were all over the place, and the defence was as bad as ever. Yet, in bizarre Toon tradition, by half-time the score was level. First Jermaine Jenas headed his first goal for the club. Then Alan Shearer drove in a penalty after Craig Bellamy was tripped in the box.

But normal service was resumed after the break, with comical defending allowing George Ndah to score the winner. After the final whistle, Bellamy displayed his Premiership shirt badge to the Wolves fans and mouthed, 'This is what it's all about'. But the chances of actually winning the Premiership were slim, and the chances of winning the FA Cup, after this dismal showing, were out of the window.

Still, 'it's only a game'. Bollocks it is. It is undeniably important. Every football fan will have had, at one point in their life, a well-meaning friend or relative try to console them after a defeat with the words, 'Never mind, it's only a game'. Wrong. It's a way of life. Never tell a member of the Toon Army, 'It's only a game'. Football can't be only a game. Because no game matters enough to break your heart.

Mark Oliver from Bradford via Lobley Hill admits to having 'hoyed the yellow pages at the girlfriend after "it's only a game" comments'. This is the same Mark Oliver who claims that he doesn't love Newcastle United as much as he loves Jesus. God help his girlfriend if she ever says, 'It's only a religion.'

Darrel Birkett from Newcastle says, 'It's not just supporting. It's part of you. Nothing stirs so many emotions. Nothing even comes close. It's more than just being a fan. It's a way of life.'

RK from Japan by way of Durham loses all ability to communicate after defeats. Possibly he's overestimating the Japanese ability to understand Geordie.

Adrian Longley from Gateshead says, 'Everything is focussed on Newcastle results and performances. Every weekend is either great or terrible dependant on the result.'

'The feeling when we win cannot be surpassed,' says Ian Robson from Wallsend. 'And never do I feel as bad as when we lose. But I love it. I'm proud to be a Geordie.'

Now surely was the time for the Newcastle United Football Club museum to be boarded up like an old abandoned mine. Now I love the Toon more than Joanie loves Chachie, but United's relentless run of build-our-hopes-up, knock-em-down campaigns had forced me to consider that the club would never win anything ever again.

At the start of the season, while my drinking buddies planned an extravagant Double celebration, I had refused to speculate on the possibility that Newcastle might actually win something. Only now, after it had become apparent we would probably not be seeing Alan Shearer hold aloft anything big and silver this season, did I realise that I really did think United would win a tin cup this season, for the first time since that 1969 European triumph that I'm too young to remember. If United were going to avoid finishing this season trophyless they would need a Premiership or Champions League miracle.

In the aftermath of United's FA Cup exit, Shaun Custis, the chief sports writer at national rag *The Sun*, launched an astonishing attack on the Toon Army. In a piece entitled, 'Meet the Magpies that don't like silver,' Custis asked, 'What have the following clubs got in common: Stoke, Wolves, Nottingham Forest, Norwich, Oxford, Luton, Leicester, Sunderland, West Ham, Ipswich, Southampton and Coventry. Answer: They have all won a trophy since Newcastle United last lifted one.'

'Ludicrous, isn't it?' continued Custis. 'The Magpies are supposedly one of the giants of the game and it's 34 YEARS since they held a major piece of silverware. That came in 1969 when they lifted the Inter-Cities Fairs Cup, the forerunner to the UEFA Cup.'

Of course, the hack's facts were correct, although the side's placing upon publication of his article at fourth in the Premiership and in the last 16 of the Champions League would suggest that United certainly remain one of the giants of the game. Then Custis turned on the fans.

'The abiding memories that football fans have of the Geordies is failure. The honours board in the official club history lists such stunning successes as the Anglo-Italian Cup of 1973, the Texaco Cup in '74 and '75 and 1983's Japan Cup. And the saddest part about it is the supporters remember them all with fond affection.'

Horseshit. It's extremely doubtful that any football fans are stupid enough to regard a team in Newcastle's position as failures. And no Newcastle fan regards the tin pots listed by Custis as 'stunning successes'. The Toon Army dismiss the Anglo-Italian, Texaco, and Japan Cups as nothing more than footnotes. We openly admit we have not won anything since 1969 – a long and lonely wait for silverware. But so what? If you offered the supporters of any of the 12 clubs mentioned by Custis the chance to swap their trophy to stand fourth in the Premiership and in the last 16 of the Champions League it is a safe bet that they would bite your hand off.

'Ladies and gentleman,' finished Custis, 'I give you the greatest under-achievers in English football history.'

In fact, Newcastle United began season 2002-03 as the 8th most successful English football side of all time, based on trophies won. Sunderland were 12th. Nevertheless, Sunderland fans leapt upon Custis' shoddy work, and e-mails began to circulate under the slightly misleading headline, 'The Truth!' Unfortunately for Sunderland fans, this only served to reinforce the stereotype of bitter Mackems.

'The greatest under-achievers in English football history'? To borrow a quote from Bart Simpson; 'Underachievers and proud of it, man.'

Newcastle United cannot win in London. That is the maxim, although last season, when the media feverishly leapt upon it, Newcastle smashed the London 'hoodoo' and reached the pinnacle of the Premier League with a magnificent victory at Arsenal. And what did the *Evening Chronicle* put on the front page the following day? Goalscorers O'Brien, Shearer, or Robert celebrating? A huge commemorative 'cut out and keep' league table? A campaign to crown Bobby Robson as the king of Newcastle? No sir. Page one (and pages two and three) featured comedy spoon bender Uri Gellar.

For, the *Chronicle* claimed, by way of running around Highbury several times, it was Gellar who had won the game, and not a titanic effort from Bobby and the boys. And this was not the first time the paper had used mumbo-jumbo to try to end the London curse. They had already sought the help of a witch doctor, and forced Alan Oliver to sell his soul to Beelzebub (possibly). But it was Wacko Jacko's best man who finally came up trumps. Gellar, who, around the same time, told TV's *Richard and Judy* he knew where terrorist leader Osama Bin Laden was hiding but 'couldn't possibly say any more', had smashed the London hoodoo.

Forgive me if I sound sceptical. But I don't believe in hoodoos. The plain fact is that Newcastle hadn't won in London for an age because they hadn't been any good for ages. For the record, I don't believe in superstition either. The wearing of lucky underpants is not for me. I believe in science and logic, and that you make your own luck through hard graft. And the London hoodoo was broken by a battling performance, not Uri bloody Gellar.

My only concession to a set routine around football is to play simulations of upcoming fixtures on the PlayStation 2 in a futile effort to predict the score. Futile because the actual score is very rarely 8-6. However, I am proud to announce that Newcastle United have won every single domestic and European trophy since the invention of the home computer – all in the comfort of my front room. From Match Day on the Spectrum, through Sensible Soccer on the Amiga, to Pro Evolution Soccer on the PlayStation 2, Newcastle have reigned supreme.

Other members of the Toon Army, however, take superstitions very seriously. 'Some of us only drink lager before a game, while others only drink Brown Ale,' says Anth Nicholson of North Shields. 'We all have various lucky shirts socks and underpants. And we dare not go through any turnstile but lucky number 64, and even use the same toilet for our pre-match pee!'

It was less the London hoodoo that worried me ahead of Newcastle's trip to West Ham, and more the fact that the Hammers had failed to win a Premiership home game all season. Newcastle, having won only twice on their travels this season, looked as likely as any team to change all that.

Making his West Ham debut at the Boleyn Ground was Lee Bowyer, who, when a Leeds United player, had been cleared of involvement in the assault on an Asian student in Leeds city centre. Hammers fans seemed torn on the issue, and those holding anti-racism placards clashed with those wearing Bowyer shirts outside the ground. Inside, another ridiculous band of cheerleaders (welcomed by the PA announcer with the line, 'Please welcome the Hammerettes. It's bitterly cold, and I'm sure they'd appreciate a warm hand on their entrance') failed to enliven the atmosphere.

Bowyer received a very muted welcome, and, as the match got under way, delivered very little on the pitch. Instead, with Alan Shearer suspended due to Uriah Rennie's dislike for him, it was Craig Bellamy who opened the scoring, meeting a Jermaine Jenas cut back, with a smart turn and finish. But characteristic defensive errors allowed Joe Cole and Jermaine Defoe to put West Ham in front by half-time. However, with both sides flattering to deceive, it was a moment of magic that decided the result. Young Jermaine Jenas controlled a clearance on his chest and whacked an unstoppable 20-yard left-foot volley past West Ham's David James. It was a goal the quality of which the game scarcely deserved. The match ended 2-2, and Newcastle gratefully took a point, but, as the media were quick to remind us, our side had once again failed to win in London.

During Sunderland's dire goalless home draw with Blackburn, the Mackems cheered the half-time announcement that their relegation rivals West Ham were beating Newcastle. Of course, Newcastle actually did

Sunderland a favour by fighting back to draw at the Boleyn Ground – news that was met with groans at the Stadium of Light. Amazingly, the Mackems would rather have seen West Ham win and increase Sunderland's probability of relegation than see Newcastle take any points.

Before the home match against Manchester City on 18 January, Alan Shearer was presented with the Premiership Goal of the Month trophy for his strike against Everton to fine applause from the home fans. And then, straight from the kick-off, the big man notched up yet another record.

Man City centred, and Steve Howey played the ball straight back to stand-in goalkeeper Carlo Nash. But Nash's first touch was terrible. He knocked the ball straight at the onrushing Shearer, who controlled and fired home with his left foot. There were 10 seconds on the clock, meaning Shearer equalled the record for the fastest ever Premiership goal, sharing it with Ledley King of Spurs. Chalk it up.

Man City offered little by way of comeback. Jenas and Dyer easily controlled the midfield, and the under-fire Robert turned in a thoroughly decent performance, although it was noticeable that several of his teammates seemed reluctant to pass to him. The Toon Army regaled former player Sylvain Distin, who left because he wanted more money, with 'One greedy bastard'. And we raised the roof when, at half-time, the United hero presented on the pitch was none other than Peter Beardsley. Kevin Keegan got a muted reception, save for a rousing chorus of 'Keegan, Keegan, what's the score?' belted out shortly after Bellamy had made it 2-0 from a Robert cross half way through the second half.

After this comfortable 2-0 win, Newcastle sat third in the league, behind Arsenal and Manchester United, but with a game in hand. With home games to come against Arsenal, Man United, and Chelsea, it became clear that Newcastle were by no means out of the Premiership title race quite yet.

In midweek, Bolton were the visitors to St James', and United were out for revenge after the disappointing defeat at the Reebok. In the pub before the match, we agreed that another seven goal-thriller was not required. One-nil would do. And 1-0 it was. After 20 minutes, Bellamy cut the ball back from the byline, and Jenas nutmegged the keeper to score. Newcastle dominated the first half, putting together some neat passing moves, but Bolton took charge in the second half. With substitute Campo controlling things from midfield, Wanderers did everything but score. Newcastle's 11th consecutive home win was not the most convincing of the lot. But neither team nor crowd buckled under the pressure, and another satisfying three points were in the bag.

Uri Gellar was conspicuous by his absence as Newcastle headed back to the big smoke to face Tottenham Hotspur on the 29th. Also absent were Steve Caldwell and Aaron Hughes – both laid low by flu. So Bobby Robson brought in the fit-again Titus Bramble to shore up the defence. And it was a masterstroke. Spurs rarely threatened, particularly after their striker Robbie Keane left the field with an injury. Newcastle played a patient game, and it looked like they would be returning to Tyneside with a hard-earned point.

Then, in the very last minute, Bramble surged out of defence with the ball. Pushing to the edge of the Spurs box, he laid the ball off to Bellamy. His driven shot was parried by keeper Kasey Keller, only to fall at the feet of Jermaine Jenas. Young Jenas, the Toon's teenage scoring sensation, bundled the ball into the back of the net – 1-0. The final whistle blew, the Toon Army were ecstatic, and the odious Glenn Hoddle legged it down the tunnel. The Spurs manager moaned about an offside decision in his post-match interview, stating that a disallowed Gus Poyet effort was 'definitely onside'. TV replays proved that Hoddle was 'definitely bonkers'.

As United moved into second place in the table, ahead of Manchester United and just behind Arsenal, Bobby Robson spoke about his side's title chances, saying, 'Arsenal, Manchester United, and Chelsea still have to come to Newcastle, so it will be interesting.'

Suddenly, the title was on. If Newcastle could beat the other three challengers at home they could effectively put Man United and Chelsea out of the race, setting up a head-to-head against Arsenal. Optimism was high, and the events of the next few days helped raise it further.

Newcastle had been chasing Leeds and England centre back Jonathan Woodgate for some time. Leeds were in desperate financial trouble and needed to sell star players. But, when Kevin Keegan finally succeeded in securing the protracted transfer of Robbie Fowler from Leeds to Man City, and with the closure of the transfer window rapidly approaching, it seemed that Leeds would hold on to Woodgate. Still, however, rumours persisted. On the day of the Spurs game, Toon chairman Freddy Shepherd was seen leaving a Chelsea hotel with Leeds chairman Peter Ridsdale. The following morning, the deal exploded into life.

The text message read, 'WOODY BID ACCEPTED!' Phone calls and websites and Radio 5 were scoured for information. And, at 10.30, it was confirmed. Leeds had accepted a bid from Newcastle of £9 million for Woodgate. Leeds at first denied the story, being under intense pressure from their disgruntled fans and from boss Terry Venables not to sell the player. But by mid-afternoon, Freddy Shepherd had confirmed the deal. Woodgate drove up to St James' through heavy snow, and completed the signing on the following day.

Much was made of the uproar from Leeds fans as their club sold another key player following the sales of Rio Ferdinand, Robbie Keane, Lee Bowyer, and Fowler. The Toon Army were delighted with the signing, but we knew how Leeds fans were feeling. After all, it hadn't been so long ago that Newcastle United had been in the habit of selling their best players. The sales of Waddle, Beardsley, and Gascoigne had led to a tumble into the Second Division and a long and miserable period of rotten football. Now, conversely, the signing of Woodgate could herald a concerted push for silverware.

At £9 million, Woodgate became the club's third biggest signing after £15 million Alan Shearer and £9.5 million Laurent Robert. The signing was the most expensive made by any club in the world during the transfer window. How far we had come. Huge receipts from our Champions League adventure had allowed the club to cement a deserved place among football's powerful elite. First you get the money, then you get the power, then you get the trophies.

Woodgate impressed in his first press conference as a United player. 'Newcastle have got a great young set of talented players and a great manager – and hopefully we'll bring trophies to the club,' he said. 'There are plenty of reasons for me to come here. The players, the manager and 55,000 supporters for each game. I am really excited at the new challenge of joining Newcastle United – one of Europe's biggest clubs.'

'This is a club that is pushing for the highest honours in the league and Europe and I hope to be part of something special over the next few years.'

His words sent a tingle down the spine of the trophy-starved Toon Army. Tipped as a future England captain, surely this confident 23-year-old would one day take the Toon armband from Alan Shearer, and lead United's bright young things – Bramble, Viana, Jenas, Dyer, Bellamy, Ameobi, Chopra and all – toward a glittering future.

The negative aspect to the signing was Woodgate's conviction for affray after a fight, purported by the media to be a racist attack. Woodgate responded to this in an effective, if obviously pre-scripted statement: 'The court case was a bad time for me but I'm not a racist player. Ask Michael Chopra, Harpal Singh, Kieron Dyer. They'll tell you that I am not a racist. I'm black and white.'

Then the player headed to the steps outside the stadium, where hundreds of fans had gathered to greet their new hero. Brand new 'WOODGATE 27' shirts were signed. 'Woodgate is a Geordie!' was sung. And, with United sitting second in the Premiership, the new acquisition's words rang around St James' Park: 'I believe we can win the League – why not?'

JANUARY

01 Jan 2003 Premiership	Newcastle United 1 Liverpool 0
05 Jan 2003 FA Cup	Wolverhampton Wanderers 3 Newcastle United 2
11 Jan 2003 Premiership	West Ham United 2 Newcastle United 2
18 Jan 2003 Premiership	Newcastle United 2 Manchester City 0
22 Jan 2003 Premiership	Newcastle United 1 Bolton Wanderers 0
29 Jan 2003 Premiership	Tottenham Hotspur 0 Newcastle United 1

Premiership: 2nd
FA Cup: Eliminated
Champions League Group A: 4th

CHAPTER NINE

February

UNITED were flying, second in the league and buoyed by the signing of Jonathan Woodgate. By contrast, Middlesbrough were floundering. Following an awful midweek defeat, with key players injured, and with a clutch of transfer deadline day signings yet to be integrated into the team, Boro could have been forgiven for dreading the Tyne-Tees non-derby, due to be played at their Riverside Stadium on 1 February. But the Teesside club could not be forgiven for the highly dubious methods they used to avoid the clash.

The match was postponed a full 28 hours before kick-off, despite the fact that Stockton-based referee Jeff Winter, a man with supposed Boro loyalties, deemed the pitch to be playable. The official reason given for postponement was that it would be unsafe for the game to proceed due to the amount of snow and ice on the terraces. Sky Sports reported that the decision to postpone had been taken by a safety official, and was out of the hands of the club. When said safety official was interviewed wearing a Boro overcoat various alarm bells began to ring.

In fact the weather on the day before the match had been atrocious, and, had the bad weather continued and the decision to postpone been made on the day of the match, most fans would have had no problem with it. However, with over 24 hours to go before kick-off, had Middlesbrough FC not heard of thaw? Failing that, why could they not do what near neighbours Hartlepool did and invite fans to help clear the terraces?

Claims were made by irate Boro fans, on the Friday night Century Radio Three Legends football phone-in, that their own club had 'bottled out' of playing the match. Callers were adamant that conditions around the Riverside stadium were safe, and claims were made that no request from the club was made to the council for gritting and snow clearance.

As it was, the thaw prevailed, and the Saturday morning found the Riverside in almost spring-like conditions, with barely a sliver of snow or ice in sight.

Bobby Robson was furious, as were the Newcastle fans – being deprived of a short and potentially victorious away day.

So was it spurious to suggest that the absences from the Boro side of the injured players, plus the new signings, may have had a bearing on the club's decision to postpone? The fact that Boro dismissed Newcastle's request to replay the match on the following Tuesday suggested not.

In 2003 it was ridiculous to consider that a Premiership club should call off a match due to a light dusting of snow, particularly when the pitch had been deemed playable. Boro had failed their own fans, and those of Newcastle United, and had made a mockery of the FA Premiership and its fixture list.

In an ideal world, the three points should have been awarded to Newcastle United, and Boro should have been forced to compensate travelling supporters who have shelled out for tickets and travel arrangements. As it was, the FA refused to investigate the incident, inexplicably saying it was outside of its jurisdiction.

On that Saturday, while Newcastle United kicked their heels, both Arsenal and Manchester United took victories, knocking Newcastle into third place, and knocking the wind out of black and white sails. Elsewhere,

Sunderland dropped to the bottom of the Premiership, scoring an unprecedented three own-goals in a 3-1 defeat to Charlton at the Stadium of Light. The Toon Army were disappointed with the situation forced upon Newcastle, but events in Sunderland reminded that things could have been a whole lot worse.

So the Toon Army had no football to keep them going over the weekend. This called for a big night out. Newcastle's reputation as one of the top 10 party cities in the world (it was beaten in a poll by Las Vegas) is well deserved. As a result, in addition to thousands of Geordies, partygoers from around the country and beyond descend upon the city at weekends. And visitors expecting to find run-down *Get Carter*-style pubs full of flat caps and whippets are set to be disappointed. For better or for worse, the city has been overrun with trendy bars and 'fun pubs'. When new bar Tiger Tiger opened early into the season, Geordie punters were amazed to find a velvet rope, a guest list, and a pub that didn't serve draft pints. How times change.

Luckily, there are still a handful of traditional pubs around the city where locals can sip Newcastle's own 'Broon' Ale, and students can order 'Newkey Brown', even though 'Newkey' is surely a place down South favoured by bleach-haired surfers. Much football talk is done here, and in the Haymarket's more relaxed selection of bars. But the real party is to be found elsewhere.

For a 'traditional' night out, the Bigg Market remains quite an experience. Smoke and loud music billow from bars, teenage lads with bum-fluff moustaches blow chunks in doorways, and drunken lasses in micro-skirts eagerly flash their shivering breasts at passing police vans. Hen-night parties drive through the streets in cheap limousines, the bride-to-be wearing a black bin bag with L-plates stapled to it and a hat fitted with semi-inflated condoms. Stag parties reel from pub to pub, inevitably dressed in 1970s gear, genuinely believing that they are the first to do so in the name of good humour.

Decidedly more upmarket, away from the discarded pizza boxes and vans of riot police, is the city's Quayside. The bridges are lit up at night, and the spectacular views offered by riverside pubs mean this is very much the place to be, even if you do have to stand in queues and pay £3 a pint for the privilege.

The Quayside is something of a honey-trap used to entice players to Newcastle. When Colombian striker Faustino Asprilla first arrived on Tyneside suitably attired in a fur coat during a heavy snowstorm, his interpreter took him on a tour of Newcastle, which culminated in a trip to the Quayside. Asprilla was amazed to see hordes of young women shivering in mini skirts and skimpy tops. When one girl shouted 'Tino' and flashed her G-string at him, he turned to his companion and said, 'What a town!'

Sir Bobby Robson continues to use the Quayside tactic today, saying, 'If we invite any player up to the Quayside to see the girls and then our magnificent stadium, we will be able to persuade any player to sign.'

From pubs to clubs to takeaway, football permeates the Toon Army's night out. Football talk, reflections and predictions, agreements and arguments, are par for the course. And, with the influx of visitors to the city, there is likely to be some banter with fans of other clubs. There is rarely any trouble. One of the major benefits of the city's cultural revival is that your night is now much more likely to end in a Chinese takeaway or a kebab shop rather than in the local casualty department.

And then to the taxi. Every taxi driver in Newcastle will just have had either Kieron Dyer or Craig Bellamy in the back of his cab, and therefore will be able to offer up a dubious piece of inside information. Even in a black cab at three in the morning, as the bright lights of the city centre disappear in the rear-view mirror, the talk is, inevitably, of Newcastle United Football Club.

Massive: Arsenal, top of the table, visited Newcastle, eight points behind with a game in hand, on 9 February. Should Newcastle continue their 11-match winning streak at St James' Park, then they would stand just five points behind the current champions, still with that game in hand. Should Newcastle lose, then they would stand 11 points behind Arsenal, and surely end their flirtation with the Premiership title.

The 4pm Sunday start served only to heighten the tension. We headed to the pub four hours before kick-off to watch our title rivals Manchester United take on Manchester City. The bars were packed and buzzing, and the anticipation was special and intoxicating. And, with the Toon Army's collective eye fixed on big screens across Newcastle, Man City's last-gasp equaliser sent the packed pubs into rapture. That 1-1 draw pegged back Man United to within touching distance, if Newcastle could beat Arsenal. By 4 o'clock my fingernails were gnawed back so far as to make opening a ring-pull can a complete impossibility. But the intake of pre-match alcohol had imbued in me a peculiar surge of confidence. Bets were placed, seats were taken, and, in a St James' Park fizzing with excitement, the biggest of matches, the game of the season, began.

The atmosphere in the stadium was easily the most intense of the term. The remarkable passion of the Toon Army was vocalised to the extreme as 52,000 fans bared their souls. Normally quiet sections of the crowd joined in the clamour. The noise was phenomenal.

'Newcas-tle, Newcas-tle, Newcas-tle!'

'Toon! Toon! Black and white army!'

Surely no other crowd, not even in Ancient Rome in the midst of gladiatorial combat, could make such uproar. So *Blaydon Race*s, and the Old Spice tune, and then *Local Hero*, and then the teams were out, and the game was on.

Both teams responded to the support, and the game exploded into frenzied life. Play surged from end to end like a basketball game, each side soaking up pressure, winning possession, and counterattacking with speed. The crowd's mood peaked and troughed like a stormy sea, from fevered anticipation as Newcastle attacked, to flustered apprehension as Arsenal riposted.

With new-signing Jonathan Woodgate injured, Newcastle lined up with Titus Bramble and Andy O'Brien at the back. Both stood strong to repel Arsenal's Thierry Henry and Dennis Bergkamp. At the other end, Alan Shearer and Sol Campbell engaged in a thunderous battle, fierce and bruising, and at times akin to watching some Japanese monster movie like *Godzilla v Mothra*. In midfield, Kieron Dyer and Jermaine Jenas, both named in Sven Goran Eriksson's England International squad just hours earlier, knuckled down to great effect. Dyer in particular belied his lack of size, clattering, battering, and forcing mistakes from his mighty opponent Patrick Viera. Meanwhile, Laurent Robert, matched against so many of his French compatriots, including fellow left-winger Robert Pires, was on fire. Showing the form that had mostly eluded him throughout the season, he was supremely fleet of foot, skipping past defenders, and working deadly openings.

It was Robert who created the first clear-cut chance. Surging 60 yards upfield, he outpaced the Arsenal defence and drove in a brilliant curling cross. Shearer, entangled with Campbell, poked the ball toward the far corner. But England keeper David Seaman went low to make a smart save. Then Arsenal responded. Henry's corner was headed goal-bound by Viera, and the ball struck Nol Solano's knee, ricocheted on to the crossbar, and fell to Robert Pires, who headed over from point blank range. Then another Henry cross was mistakenly headed toward his own-goal by Bramble. Shay Given, already in full flight, adjusted his neck and amazingly headed the ball over his goal. A remarkable save.

Shearer continued to combat Arsenal's defence, and was booked after an incident with the Ashley Cole and Viera. Cole had dived, and was booed for the remainder of the match. And Viera charged at Shearer with arms raised, yet was unpunished.

Then, 10 minutes before half-time, Arsenal got the crucial breakthrough. Solano and Robert had temporarily swapped wings and, when Newcastle won a throw-in in their own half, Nobby turned his back on play and trotted back to his normal position. As a result, Olivier Bernard's throw was picked up by Arsenal, and Sylvain Wiltord was able to play Henry through on goal. The Frenchman, probably the Premiership's player of the season, skipped past Given and made it 1-0.

When the half-time announcer inexplicably played The Flaming Lips'

Yoshimi Battles The Pink Robots Part 1 rather than the usual Pop Idol drivel during the interval it should have indicated that an extraordinary second half lay in wait. Sir Bobby replaced the uninspiring Solano with a fit-again Gary Speed. Speedo, back in action just five weeks after a hernia operation, was welcomed with a standing ovation. And it was his pass that led to the equaliser, although all the plaudits had to go to goal-scorer Robert. Dribbling through the Arsenal defence, Robert lashed an unstoppable left-foot curler past Seaman. The Toon Army's pent up anticipation detonated into a huge explosive roar. 'Yessssss!'

But, five minutes later, the roar became one of anger. After being booked for a hard tackle, Robert had the ball kicked at him at point blank range by Dennis Bergkamp. Adjudging that Robert had deliberately blocked Bergkamp's free-kick, referee Neale Barry showed the Frenchman a second yellow card and sent him off.

It had been a brilliant game up to that point, a fantastic free flowing advert for British football. The only sour point had been Barry's niggling decisions, pointless pickiness like refusing to play advantages from free-kicks. Now Barry had ruined the biggest match of the season. There was unremitting fury from around the ground. Had the referee used any common sense he could have realised that Robert could not have moved out of the way of the ball, giving him a ticking off at worst. Instead, Newcastle were down to 10 men against the Premiership champions. The distraught Robert, effervescent on the day and surely the potential match winner, was applauded from the pitch.

A tactical shuffle saw Craig Bellamy pulled back into midfield. And, backed by the Toon Army's wall of sound, Newcastle proceeded to batter Arsenal back on to their heels. But gross stupidity from the officials continued to hamper proceedings. Aaron Hughes shielded a ball out for a goal-kick and was then clattered by the increasingly irritating Cole. The linesman made Newcastle take a free-kick on the touchline, even though the ball had already gone out of play before the foul was committed.

Then, in stoppage time, and with Newcastle in the ascendancy, Kieron

Dyer went down with cramp. And Neale Barry sneeringly, insultingly, made a 'time-wasting' gesture at him. The young kid had ran his heart out for over 90 minutes, and was now being accused of cheating by the very person who had ruined the game as a contest. Barry refused to allow Dyer treatment, and forced him to leave the pitch, where he lay in agony until the end of the match. The crowd around me were spitting venom, surging forward, almost holding each other back from charging on to the pitch to do something unspeakable to the detestable Barry.

Still, now with just nine men on the field, it was Newcastle who almost nicked it, with Bellamy's curling cross-shot being superbly tipped over by Seaman. But it wasn't quite to be. Barry blew the final whistle and hurried from the pitch under a torrent of dog's abuse. The players, meanwhile, were cheered from the field. Arsenal, too, took considerable applause. Although Newcastle had outplayed them, the champions had held off a Premiership rival to take a vital point. For Newcastle, one point was surely not enough to sustain the title challenge. Realistically, the dream was over for another year. But the disappointment could not eclipse the pride in the performance of the team. They had, to a man, given more than could have been asked and, despite the referee, they had more than matched Arsenal to point to a thrilling, brilliant future.

In the pub we sat, drained of energy, and discussed the match in damaged voices. There was still great anger at the referee and at Dennis Bergkamp. But the overwhelming feeling was of pride in our team. We supped a couple of pints and headed home, taking memories of a tumultuous match with us into the night.

One of the many brilliant things about football is the fact that everything can change in a split second. The Toon Army have experienced many of these moments in recent times, from Craig Bellamy's last-gasp winner in Rotterdam, back to David Kelly's club-saving goal against Portsmouth in 1992. These were moments that not only defined their seasons but also helped shape the history of the club and, by association, changed the lives of its supporters.

Of course, these defining moments don't always change football fans' lives in a positive way. Rob Lee's beautiful equalising header in the Wembley FA Cup semi-final of 2000 was voted in the Toon Army survey one of the greatest ever Toon-supporting moments. But, seconds later, it was a defining moment from Chelsea's Gus Poyet that really counted, with his winning goal rendering Rob's strike useless and effectively ending Newcastle's season.

In the movie *Back to the Future*, Marty McFly went back in time to make sure his Mam and Dad got together, and, in the BBC TV show, *Doctor Who* regularly went back in time to stop lumbering extras in shoddy costumes from taking over the world. What if Newcastle fans could travel back in time somehow to change for the better moments that mucked up our lives?

If it was me in the blue police box and overlong knitted scarf, first I'd nip back to Hereford, 1972, and clip Ronnie Radford's heels just as he was lining up his FA Cup strike. Personally, I'm too young to have been directly affected by that goal, but at least it would stop the BBC from replaying it every five minutes.

The 1974 Cup Final defeat through to, if we're being honest, just about the whole of the 1980s, were not so much moments as an entire era of pathetic underachievement. Not even *Quantum Leap's* Scott Bakula, the do-gooding lady-loving time traveller, could have fixed that mess.

So the next stop is St James' Park, 1990, the Sunderland play-off, and a *Doctor Who*-style mission to stop lumbering Eric Gates in a shoddy poison dwarf costume from scoring for the Mackems against the Toon. Gates's shot is blocked, Newcastle's Mark McGhee's shot is deflected in instead of hitting the post, Sunderland's Marco Gabbiadini's shot is blocked, McGhee's second shot is deflected in instead of being saved by big-nosed Sunderland keeper Tony Norman, and no one feels the need to invade the pitch. Okay, that's five moments, but you get the idea. Newcastle get promoted, and Sunderland spend eternity languishing in the Second Division.

Then, fast-forward to 1996 and the Premier League title race. Manchester United striker Eric Cantona's shot at St James' is saved, and one of Newcastle's many chances is bundled into the net. Then, on the last day of that season, weasley Middlesbrough are coerced into actually turning up for, and winning, their match against Manchester United. Newcastle win the league by two clear points. Geddin.

Next, 1997, and Kevin Keegan's resignation. Appear as a Charles Dickens-style 'Ghost of Seasons Future' and warn the board about the folly of appointing Dalglish or Gullit. The Robson revolution begins two years early, everything is rosy, and, in all probability, by now we are several leaps and bounds ahead of the likes of Arsenal in the league, and, most likely, have eclipsed Real Madrid in Europe.

And then to Wembley in 2000 to stand on Gus Poyet's toes as he looks to head his winning goal. He fails to score, Newcastle heads don't go down, and we go on to win the game and progress to the final.

Not all bad Newcastle United moments could be changed, though. There is a time travel theory, probably only properly understood by the likes of Stephen Hawking, which says that any tiny change made in the past will massively change the present. So if you go back in time and step on a butterfly you will return to the present to find you've wiped out the human race, or something or other. By the same token, if you went back to 1999, gave Ruud Gullit a slap, and forced him to play Shearer and Ferguson in that famous match against Sunderland, it may result in a rain-lashed victory. But the consequences could see Gullit keep his job, ruling out the appointment of Bobby Robson. By making a small improvement in the past you'd have created a massive deterioration in the present. Bad idea.

Before we get too waylaid by sci-fi mumbo jumbo, we should perhaps return to reality. The moment that all of this has been leading up to is the sending off of Laurent Robert against Arsenal. The lad was on fire. He'd scored a brilliant goal, and was surely destined to be the match winner. There were no arguments about his first booking. But the second booking was diabolical. And I'm afraid that the 'letter of the law' rubbish spouted by the press in the aftermath of the match just didn't wash.

Compare the match to the Man United v Arsenal FA Cup-tie, televised live in the following week. Manchester's Ruud Van Nistelrooy committed an awful high foul just seconds after being booked. And Paul Scholes blasted the ball at an Arsenal player's crown jewels, also having already been booked. Referee Jeff Winter clearly considered that he had already booked the two players and decided not to spoil a good game by sending them off.

The Robert incident was much less serious. His half-hearted attempt to block Bergkamp's free-kick was non-violent and commonplace. But Neale Barry decided to adhere to the 'letter of the law'. He spoiled the biggest game of the season, effectively stopping Newcastle from taking the three points and halting any realistic chance they had of winning the Premiership title.

When your team don't perform well, as happened away at Man United and Bolton earlier in the season, or are comprehensively outplayed, as they were at home to Inter Milan, you hold your hands up and accept it. But when split second moments spoil all your team's good work, you find it very hard to bear. If only we could travel back in time somehow...

The Champions League campaign restarted on 18 February with a trip to Bayer Leverkusen. The German side had dispensed of the services of their coach just days before, following a huge slide in form. Last season's Champions League finalists, Bundesliga runners up, and German Cup finalists, were now facing domestic relegation. Even without the suspended Shearer and Bellamy, around 3,000 members of the Toon Army travelled to Germany confident of victory.

Much of the Toon Army contingent decided to stay in nearby Cologne rather than the rather dreary Leverkusen, where the only bright light was a huge neon 'Bayer' pharmaceuticals logo presiding over the town. Much drinking was done, but the llamas wandering around the streets were quite real and not alcohol-induced hallucinations. 'It's Llama Lua Lua!' quipped one Geordie wag.

Inside the small but modern BayArena stadium, the Toon Army were stuck behind a net, but ceiling-mounted heaters were a welcome sight. The Bayer fans seemed resigned to defeat, and, naturally, the Toon Army won the vocal contest. The Bayer fans were offered 'You're going down with the Cottbus!', in reference to their precarious Bundesliga position.

On the day of Sir Bobby Robson's 70th birthday (and Jermaine Jenas' 20th) the manager was regaled with renditions of 'Happy Birthday Sir Bobby." (Bobby had earlier remarked of his wife Elsie's arrangements for his birthday: 'I don't think she knows I'm in Germany because we play Bayer Leverkusen that night. She might have arranged a dinner party. I will have to tell her. She doesn't know. Honestly.')

On the field, Bayer's new manager made eight changes to his side. Clearly his priority was league survival. Within five minutes, Newcastle highlighted the Germans' problems. Lomana Lua Lua escaped down the right, twisted away from his man, and clipped in a good cross, which was coolly headed home by Shola Ameobi. Ten minutes later it was two. This time, Shola leapt on to a loose ball, powered past his man, and rifled in a low shot. The stand-in strikers, and Shola in particular, were performing magnificently. The 'Shola Cokey' filled the night air: 'You put your left leg in…'

But Bayer weren't dead and buried yet. On 25 minutes, Franca placed a neat finish over Shay Given to pull a goal back for Leverkusen. Newcastle responded quickly. A great Robert cross from the left was volleyed home by Lua Lua. Cue the somersaults. Newcastle were 3-1 up before half-time, away from home, in the Champions League. 'Geordies in the Champions League' segued into 'Sunderland in the Nationwide'.

The second half was less eventful, and there were no further goals. Sir Bobby had received the best possible present on his 70th birthday – a fantastic away victory at club football's very highest level.

Sir Bobby Robson's footballing achievements range farther and wider than any other British manager in history. After a fine playing career, during which he established himself as an England international midfielder, Robson began his managerial work at Vancouver Royals in 1967. He then returned to England to manage Fulham, the club he had served so well as a player, and then Ipswich, winning the FA Cup and the UEFA Cup. As England manager, he took the national side to memorable World Cups in 1986 and

1990. Then he moved abroad, winning the Dutch League twice with PSV Eindhoven, having a successful spell at Porto, and then winning the European Cup-winners' Cup with Barcelona.

But, setting aside his remarkable record of achievements, the thing that really sets Sir Bobby Robson apart is his measure as a man. He is loved and respected by Newcastle supporters like a favourite Grandad. The Toon Army were hoping that Sir Bobby could bring silverware to Newcastle before time, inevitably, caught up with the best-loved man in football.

With the team in such great form and with the acquisition of Jonathan Woodgate fresh in minds, the Toon Army headed to Leeds United on Saturday 22nd in buoyant mood. Leeds is rarely a particularly welcoming place to the football fan, and previous visits have involved various unsavoury incidents, many involving the notorious underpass leading to the Elland Road stadium. But today the Leeds fans were in no mood to offer any resistance, vocal or otherwise. Enduring a torrid season of underachievement and the sale of their star players appeared to have left them completely demoralised.

After the short drive down, I parked up, paying £3 to a dodgy-looking bloke for the privilege of parking on a piece of wasteland, as is the norm on away trips, and we headed up to the stadium past the masses of silent Leeds fans.

'Woodgate is a Geordie!' sang the Toon Army, along with a tribute to the under-fire Leeds chairman; 'Peter Ridsdale is our friend – he sold Woodgate! Sold us Woodgate on the cheap…' The Leeds fans did briefly come to life at one point, during a tongue-in-cheek Toon Army rendition of 'Sack the board!' applauding and joining in.

And if the Leeds fans were subdued, the Leeds players were virtually catatonic. Only young forward Alan Smith appeared to have any fight in him – demonstrated quite literally by way of several bad challenges. Otherwise, Newcastle dominated, even without Woodgate who did not play against his former club as stipulated in the terms of his transfer.

First, Robert clipped a ball to Shearer on the edge of the area. The skipper controlled it and played in Kieron Dyer, who lashed a left-foot shot past the Leeds keeper. After half-time, Dyer made it two, showing clever feet to manoeuvre in the box and drive low into the bottom corner. Then, a Robert free-kick was easily headed home by Shearer. The big man also had a perfectly decent goal ruled out for offside. But 3-0 it remained, and the victory could be placed alongside the best of the season.

Particularly impressive was the performance of the much-maligned defence. Woodgate would come into contention for the next league game, and the talk in the car on the way home was of how he could be accommodated into the team. With Bramble and O'Brien performing magnificently in the centre of defence, and Hughes and the returning Griffin nullifying the opposition at full-back, Sir Bobby would have a problem deciding who should make way for Woodgate and the back-from-suspension Bernard.

Bayer Leverkusen were undeniably rubbish. They'd proved that in the BayArena in the previous week. But, on a slightly subdued Champions League night during which St James' Park welcomed its millionth supporter of the season through the turnstiles, they still had to be beaten. Within 11 minutes that job was effectively done. First Alan Shearer headed in a superb Gary Speed cross. Then a Shola Ameobi cross was deflected and, again, headed home by Shearer. The Germans threatened to fight back, but Shay Given saved a poor Neuville penalty halfway through the first half. But our chosen centre back pairing of Titus Bramble and Steve Caldwell had little to deal with.

It was 3-0 before half-time, when Kieron Dyer was barged in the box and Shearer smashed the resulting penalty into the top left-hand corner of the goal. The couple of hundred German fans in attendance did have something to cheer in the second half. After some good work by Basturk, Babic placed a neat lob over Given to score a fine goal. But there was zero chance of a comeback.

The match ended 3-1, and the Toon Army's Champions League dream rolled onward and upward. Now, despite the awful start to the second stage, progress in the competition was firmly in Newcastle's hands. A win in Milan followed by a win at home against Barcelona would put us through to the quarter-finals. Conversely, defeat in Milan would mean elimination.

09 Feb 2003 Premiership	Newcastle United 1 Arsenal 1
18 Feb 2003 Champions League	Bayer Leverkusen 1 Newcastle United 3
22 Feb 2003 Premiership	Leeds United 0 Newcastle United 3
26 Feb 2003 Champions League	Newcastle United 3 Bayer Leverkusen 1

Premiership: 3rd
Champions League Group A: 3rd

CHAPTER TEN

March

IT WAS with a mixture of amusement and annoyance that we found ourselves stuck behind a group of Chelsea fans while waiting to order our pre-match pint before the Saturday lunchtime match against the Londoners. From the bemused look on the barman's face it was almost certainly the first time anyone had ever said to him, 'Give me a light ale, and stick some lime in it.' The same punter then proceeded to order an entire round of drinks individually, requesting and paying for eight strange and obscure drinks slowly and separately, much to the consternation of the growing throng behind him. Eventually we procured our pints and began to look forward to another titanic top of the table tussle.

The media had long excluded Newcastle, yet included Chelsea, among the Premiership front-runners, despite our lead over the Londoners in the league. Victory today would put Newcastle well clear of the Blues and effectively end their interest in the League. Jonathan Woodgate would make his Newcastle debut in defence alongside Andy O'Brien, and Hugo Viana would come into the left side of midfield for the suspended Laurent Robert.

After half an hour, the Toon Army found out why Nobby Solano had been hitting the first defender with his crosses all season. Chelsea's first defender, Jimmy Floyd Hasselbaink, powered a header into his own net. But, before half-time, Chelsea drew level. A Hasselbaink corner was deflected out to Frank Lampard, and the England midfielder lobbed the ball past Shay Given. Referee Jeff Winter, fresh from his involvement in the Middlesbrough postponement scandal, was having a nightmare. At half-time he was serenaded from the pitch with, 'You're just a fat Smoggie bastard!' the The orange-skinned Winter unwisely responded with a theatrical yawn. However, Newcastle had been the better side, and, 10 minutes into the second half, Viana cleverly delayed a pass, then played in Olivier Bernard who placed a neat finish over Chelsea keeper Carlo Cudicini.

The match finished 2-1, and the lunchtime kick-off allowed the Toon Army an earlier than usual post-match drinking session. The victory put Newcastle United level on points with second-placed Manchester United, and spirits in the pub were sky-high. Many drinks were supped, and we followed the plight of Sunderland, going down 1-0 at Fulham, via pub TV screens.

As the sun went down and Saturday night partygoers came out to play, merry black and whites mingled with glad rags on a night on which everything was alright with the world.

The postponed non-derby match at Middlesbrough's Riverside stadium finally took place on the evening of 5 March, and, despite our team being in the ascendancy, few Newcastle fans were particularly looking forward to the trip. Middlesbrough is an awful place, largely because of the engulfing clouds of smog emitted by the town's chemical plants. Despite protestations that the bellowing chimneys spit out nothing but steam, the air is noticeably thick and grimy.

With reference to Boro's 'Smoggies', Newcastle fans have, in previous seasons, turned up wearing chemical suits and masks. However, this time the police issued a stern warning that chemical masks would not be allowed into the stadium as they would, and I quote, 'increase the likelihood of a terrorist attack.' So they would not, perhaps acceptably in an era of escalating international terrorism, create the illusion of a terrorist attack, but would actually 'increase the likelihood' of an attack.

So we boarded our supporters' coaches outside St James's Park at 5.30 in the afternoon, and drove to a lay-by outside Middlesbrough where the police boarded and searched for chemical masks and booze. Then we headed past the spewing factories and on to the tin-pot Riverside stadium, actually arriving in time for a pre-match pint, having missed the kick-off in previous seasons due to over-zealous policing.

After the original fixture had been disgracefully postponed due to non-existent snow, rubbish local radio DJ and Boro PA announcer Mark Paige 'cleverly' played *Let It Snow* in the run-up to kick-off. Excitingly, we had arrived on Boro's 'Flag Day', a special event at which six or seven spectators waved small banners in time to loud dance music. Paige encouraged the Boro fans to perform an embarrassing Mexican wave, and then berated an eight-year-old Newcastle fan for losing a penalty shoot out to a Boro fan twice his size.

Middlesbrough ran out to the very rubbish *Pigbag* tune, to much derision from the Toon Army. Predictably, Boro fielded a team containing five or six players who would not have played had the original fixture been honoured. The match was awful, as was the performance of referee Andy D'Urso. Boro fans vented their hatred at Newcastle fans, and the Toon Army responded with 'You're just a small town in Yorkshire!' On the pitch, Newcastle managed no shots on target. Half an hour from time, a bad foul on Jermaine Jenas went unpunished. D'Urso waved play on, and Geremi found himself free to head Boro's winner.

After the final whistle, the Boro fans left the stadium singing 'We beat the scum 1-0'. We trooped to our coaches, sat waiting for a half-hour, then set off in a slow-moving police convoy which inexplicably headed south for 40 minutes. The match finished at 9.30, and we arrived back in Newcastle just before 12. That lengthy journey gave us plenty of time to reflect upon a painful defeat that had surely, finally, scuppered our title dreams.

With so much happening at St James', it seemed daft to devote time to thinking about the Mackems. But, when Howard Wilkinson was sacked on 10 March after surely one of the very worst managerial performance in footballing history (four wins in 27 games), it was impossible not to look back upon Wilko's so-short reign, and, in particular, his always amusing post-match comments.

Despite winning less than 15 per cent of his matches, Wilko claimed to be in 'profound shock' after his sacking. It wasn't the only time his thoughts had been completely at odds with the reality of the world around him. After Fulham defeated his side 1-0 in the previous week, Wilko said, 'I got what I asked for from my players – and if you list the ingredients necessary to win a match, most of them were there.' Apparently Wilkinson makes a mean omelette, too. He has all of the ingredients necessary to make an omelette, except, of course, for the eggs.

After three Sunderland own-goals gave Charlton a 3-1 victory at the Stadium of Light, Wilko unleashed a verbal pearler: 'What we did show is that the team can play here at the Stadium of Light. By the middle of the second half we had got that monkey off our backs.' It seemed Wilko genuinely thought his side had achieved something by capitulating against Charlton. There was more to come: 'I've heard people talking about the inevitability of whatever, but nothing is inevitable. I believe that the fans' cheers were genuine not ironic. The result looks bad, but we have lost a game – we were not beaten.'

After being beaten, by which I mean losing, to Southampton 1-0 at home in the previous week, Wilko had been equally confident. 'I believe we can stay up,' he said. 'I know the difference between what I saw tonight and what we can be.'

Obviously a supreme optimist, Howard had not even included Sunderland in his relegation calculations because he believed they were certain to stay up. 'I would say relegation is three from four because we are already out of it in my mind,' he said in the run up to the Mackems v Boro match. That was Sunderland, very rock bottom of the Premiership, 'already out' of the relegation battle. Wilkinson continued, 'When I look at our fixtures thankfully they are against teams around us, which makes them better fixtures. I believe we are going to get out of it and I am not too bothered who else is going to get out of it.' He failed to realise that if everyone else got 'out of it', Sunderland would remain very much 'in it'. Boro won 3-1, but Wilko wasn't downhearted: 'I have to think only that we can get out of this trouble so long as we have the games and the points to play for.'

Sadly for Wilko, those games and points to play for ran out. Mick McCarthy was the man charged with keeping Sunderland up. His chances looked less than slim.

We set off at four am on Tuesday, 11 March, on our way to yet another game that could easily be described as the biggest in Newcastle United's recent history. Some 258 miles by road and we were at Stansted Airport. From there we flew to Milan Linate, and again the Toon Army stepped into hitherto uncharted footballing territory.

The football bounced around the Duomo Piazza, rebounding off the steps of the cathedral and looping up over the square's statues. A local in a thick sports coat stepped from his scooter and lofted the ball into the air. Two tourists in short-sleeved black and white tops challenged for a header and fell into a heap on the ground. There were 12,000 of us here. 12,000 black and whites gathered in an Italian city bedecked in rainbow flags of peace; 12,000 Geordies grasping 660ml bottles of birra outside café bars in the spring sunshine; 12,000 Toon Army soldiers in Milan to support Newcastle United FC in the Champions League match against FC Internazionale Milano.

Some Geordies had taken time to see the sights of Milan and to go shopping in the massive Galleria. Occasional black and white beer drinkers stood with white Prada shopping bags at their feet. The remainder enjoyed the relatively warm weather and the comparatively strong beer, playing football and pinochle with the locals, in fine spirit, until the over-cautious police moved in and closed the bars.

The journey to the Stadio Guiseppe Meazza, or the San Siro as it is known to football fans across the globe, was unforgettable. The Metro train was packed with Geordies, and rocked with good-natured banter. 'Geordies in the Champions League!' Bemused Inter fans had clearly never seen anything like this before. 'Have you ever seen a Mackem in Milan?' At one point, the train almost came off its rails. 'Pogo if you love the Toon!' It was brilliant – Geordies and Milanese grinning and loving every minute.

At Lotto station we boarded a shuttle bus, and the singing continued until we reached the San Siro, when something of an awed hush fell over the Toon Army. The towering stadium glowed blue and green in the night sky. More so than even the Nou Camp or the Stadio delle Alpi, this was utterly impressive. This was football's great stage, and Newcastle United and the Toon Army were here on merit.

Unfortunately, the Italian organisation was as shoddy as it had been in Turin. First the stadium stewards attempted to fit 12,000 Newcastle fans through two turnstiles in the outer perimeter fence. When, 15 minutes before kick-off, it became crushingly apparent that this was not going to work, the gates were opened, and the masses poured into the stadium. The official attendance was later given as 53,459, but this figure must have been plucked from the air, as several thousand Toon fans never passed through a turnstile, nor had their ticket stub checked or taken. The opening of the gates also allowed those without tickets to enter, including at least one Italian pickpocket. He was caught in the act by two Geordies and handed over to the police. They disinterestedly ejected him from the stadium.

Having negotiated the outer perimeter, we were then ushered through a single entrance into the stadium itself. Here things became dangerous. The Newcastle section was already full, aisles and all. Thousands of fans pushed up a small set of stairs and found themselves stuck on the gangway at the bottom of the stand. As the teams took the field and the Champions League theme filled the air, fans craned their necks for a view of the pitch and tried to prevent kids from being crushed against the stadium walls. Only the good sense of the Toon Army prevented serious injury. In the absence of designated seats, fans bunched up along rows and up aisles to allow their compatriots as much room as possible. Still, as the match kicked off, we found ourselves squashed up against a fence at the front of the stand, unable to see much at all of the action on the pitch.

Finally, after almost 10 minutes of mayhem, the police opened an empty section of the stand and allowed the displaced Toon fans in. Now high above the pitch, we could see the stadium in all its glory. The lower tiers were full, and one entire end was completely full of black and whites. The only empty seats appeared to be among the home fans in the upper tier, but still it appeared that the authorities had underestimated the attendance by around 15 to 20,000. Indeed, Toon flags peppered the stadium, and groups of Geordies could be seen all around the ground.

On the pitch, Newcastle were dominating. While stuck at the bottom of the stand we had just about managed to see Nobby Solano crash a shot against the crossbar. Now Newcastle continued to surge forward, propelled by a huge wave of support.

'We're in the San Siro! Sunderland's going down you know!'

And, on 42 minutes, the team and the Toon Army got their reward. Craig Bellamy did brilliantly on the right to cut a ball across the box, and Alan Shearer reacted first to poke the ball home. 'YESSSSSSSS!' The Toon Army toppled on top of each other like a set of dominoes, hugging and cheering and laughing. 'YESSSSSSSS!' And then, once we had picked ourselves up, and, after the obligatory 'Shearer! Shearer!', a song that brought a proud lump to the throat: 'One-nil in the San Siro! One-nil in the San Siro!'

At half-time we ate Cornettos under a scoreboard that read 'INTER 0-1 NEWCASTLE'. The Italian ices seemed bizarrely appropriate. Within minutes of the restart, however, events on and off the field darkened our mood. An Inter cross from the right was easily headed past Shay Given by Christian Vieri to put the Italians level.

At that moment, the Italian fans in the tier above us awoke from their first-half slumber with disgraceful results. Surging over the front of the stand they began to hurl bottles, coins, and stones at the Toon Army, before showering us with spittle. This continued throughout the second half, and the police did nothing to prevent it other than half-heartedly telling the offenders to sit down. One 40-plus moustachioed Italian leaned over the Toon fans for several minutes, coughing up a succession of mucky lugees, to the fury of those below. One fan just a few seats away from us was knocked unconscious by a glass bottle, but thankfully recovered after treatment from reluctant paramedics. Most worryingly of all, several Newcastle fans were burned when a huge bright red distress flare was thrown into the crowd. The Toon Army were understandably furious, but restrained themselves and responded only in song, singing, 'You're just a small town in Europe!'

Back on the pitch, the Inter players were going down like Sunderland. The Portuguese winger Conceicao was the worst offender, and the Portuguese officials rewarded his behaviour at every opportunity. And Vieri, built like the proverbial brick netty, regularly went down like an old lady in a strong wind. 'Same old Eyeties, always cheating!' sang the Toon Army, with plenty of justification. Fantastically, within two minutes, our team gave Inter the slap they deserved. Laurent Robert whipped in a great cross, Inter keeper Toldo fumbled the ball, and Shearer knocked in the rebound. 'GEDDINNNN!' 2-1 to Newcastle, and the Italian fans went strangely silent. But the Toon Army raised the volume yet again.

'2-1 in the San Siro!'

'Hey, Alan Shearer! Ooh! Aah! I wanna know how you scored that goal!'

But, with half an hour remaining, and despite the best efforts of the Newcastle team and fans, Inter managed to score another soft header courtesy, this time, of defender Cordoba. The goal came from a free-kick that should not have been, and in the final seconds, after Bellamy was denied a penalty after being brought down by Toldo, the inept referee awarded yet another crazy kick on the edge of the Newcastle penalty area. After the match it was revealed that, amid much pushing and shoving, and following the Italian fans' foul racist barracking of Titus Bramble, Christian Vieri had called Lomana Lua Lua a 'black bastard'. Thankfully, the free-kick came to nothing, the final whistle blew, and the Italians failed to steal the points.

2-2, and Newcastle were still in the Champions League, although they would need to beat Barcelona in the following week and rely on Inter to drop points in Leverkusen. The Newcastle players were applauded from the field, and the Toon Army spent a good three quarters of an hour locked in the ground, torn between pride and disappointment. Our side had played brilliantly, and were still in the competition. But victory had been so close.

We filtered out into the streets to find that there were no shuttle busses to take us back to the Metro station. So we began the long walk, with clever-clever stick-waving cops taunting us along the way. Once we reached the Metro station we found the police had cordoned it off, with no explanation or alternative given. Some fans offered the Italian police a hilarious rendition of Joe Dolce's 1981 hit *Shaddap You Face*; 'What's a matter you? Hey! Why you no respect?' After a ridiculously long wait, a few thousand fans were allowed down into the station and crammed on to what we were told would be the last train, leaving thousands stranded above. Crushed and overheated, the return journey was far less enjoyable.

Arriving back in the centre of Milan at one in the morning, two and a half hours after the final whistle, we found that every bar, café, and restaurant was closed. Milan was deserted, save for groups of Toon fans wandering the streets in search of refreshment. 'Anything open up there lads? No? Nothing up that way either.' It seemed the only establishments open in the whole of Milan were the pornography 'tents' that littered every street corner. And no, they didn't sell beer.

In the morning we found a pavement café and sipped beers while attempting to make sense of the daily Italian sports newspaper *La Gazzetta dello Sport*. It was all very *Football Italia*. Agreeing that Newcastle had controlled most of the game, the paper described Alan Shearer as 'inexorable', a simple and perfect description of the kind that you would rarely find in the British papers. It also admitted to having 'severe doubts' over the referee's refusal to award a penalty for Toldo's trip on Bellamy. In the afternoon we headed to the airport and began our long and quiet journey home.

Although UEFA would investigate claims of racism against Christian Vieri, they announced they would not take any action with respect to the racist behaviour of the Inter fans. Toon chairman Freddy Shepherd publicly thanked Inter for their hospitality. Few Toon fans could echo his sentiment. On the following Thursday, Liverpool player El Hadji Diouf spat at two Celtic fans during a UEFA Cup match. This sparked a media frenzy. In Milan thousands of Newcastle United fans had been spat at and pelted with missiles. Yet this was barely reported. UEFA eventually fined Inter £32,000 for the crowd disturbances, amounting to around £2 for each Newcastle United fan who had their European trip sullied.

Probably the most annoying aspect of our treatment in Milan was that it was by no means a one-off. Football fans are regularly treated as second-class citizens. Why should match-goers at Milan's San Siro not be treated with the same respect as opera-goers at La Scala? If an opera fan in the stalls was spat upon by someone in the circle, would no action be taken? Would opera-goers be detained in the opera house before being herded through the streets like animals? Who decided that opera fans are better people than football fans? After all, Hannibal Lector was an opera fan, not a football fan.

A consensus that was repeatedly heard on the journey home was that if the events at the San Siro had happened at St James' then the outcome would have been very different. English football fans are still regarded as hooligans, despite the fact that violence has been eliminated from the Premiership, yet continues every week in Italy's Serie A. Certainly the Toon Army are as friendly a bunch of people as you could hope to meet. There is a hooligan 'firm' known as the Newcastle Gremlins, a group of dunderheads who meet up with Sunderland's Seaburn Casuals at the Shields ferry terminal to beat each other up. But they are not football fans. They are not Toon Army. Football fans are ordinary people who love football. It's a shame that they are so often treated with disdain.

Later that week, 10 of us had the pleasure of attending a football talk-in with Sir Bobby Robson, for the benefit of Durham County Cricket Club. Aside from a misunderstanding over the meaning of the wording on the tickets (Mally thought the event was to be held in the 'Lounge Suite', and therefore neglected to tell us to wear 'lounge suits'), the evening was a pleasure from start to finish.

Showing absolutely no fatigue from his trip to Milan, and despite having to get up early the next morning to take charge of training, Bobby was energetic, hilarious, and incredibly honest. Initially sitting at a table with a microphone in front of him, he jumped to his feet, snatched up the mike, and enthusiastically recalled tales from his illustrious career. We were in stitches as Bobby told tales of the likes of Gazza and Romario, and listened intently as he gave insight into his World Cup campaigns and managerial ups and downs. But the highlights for us, natch, were the glimpses of life behind the scenes at Newcastle United. As he spoke, Bobby received a mobile phone call from club physio Derek Wright informing him that a recent injury to Kieron Dyer was not as serious as first thought.

Bobby's passion for the club was clear to see, and his opinions on the squad, and the club as a whole, left us in no doubt that he knew exactly, precisely where he wanted to take Newcastle United, and how he intended to do so. Substandard players were given short shrift. 'Where's Temuri Ketsbaia now?' he said of our rubbish former striker. 'I think he's buried. I wanted to do that to him years ago!'

The capability of the current squad was summed up honestly. Bobby revealed that he had called wayward winger Laurent Robert into his office 40 times over the season. 'When I play him, I wish I hadn't. When I don't play him, I wish I had!' There were nods of agreement from the audience. 'Remember, he scored or created 28 goals for this club last season – 28 goals! It would take Sunderland 10 years to do that!' Bobby knew what was going on. He talked about the problem of disciplining players when they have more money than they know what to do with. And he talked about the future, and who might eventually replace Alan Shearer. 'I love Shola,' said Bobby, 'and there are a couple of other pebbles on the beach.'

Bobby took questions from the audience until midnight, answering every one, even cheeky ones like, 'Do you think all England managers should have dates with Ulrika Johnson?' to which he answered, 'Yes absolutely.' But the highlight of the night came in answer to the question, 'Which do you prefer: Viana or Viagra?' Quick as a flash, Bobby replied, 'Viana on a Saturday afternoon, Viagra on a Saturday night!'

Saturday saw United travel to London to take on Charlton. With the 'London hoodoo' long since smashed, and with the amazing record of never having lost a match following a European game during the whole of Bobby Robson's reign, the signs were good. Charlton had proved themselves difficult to beat, and were pushing for a UEFA Cup place. But they had no answer for the pace of Craig Bellamy.

After half an hour, Bellamy was grabbed and kicked inside the area for a clear penalty. Alan Shearer duly dispatched the spot kick, and Newcastle took a 1-0 lead into the break. In the second half, Bellamy raced on to a Shearer header, burst into the box, and cut back a great centre. Nobby Solano easily finished from close range, and clearly signalled his appreciation of the work of Bellamy. Newcastle held out for a fairly comfortable 2-0 win. 'We always win in London!'

The following morning, the Sunday papers filled their back pages with tales of an 'Alan Shearer England U-Turn' – sensational claims that the Newcastle striker would make a return to the England squad. The stories were based upon an interview given to *The Observer* newspaper, in which Shearer was quoted as saying, 'I would be lying if I said I didn't miss playing for England. I still feel I could do a job for England, in fact I know I could.' The newspapers seized upon this comment with vigour, and Sky Sports News led their news bulletins with the story.

Those members of the press whose criticism of the man had precipitated Shearer's England retirement after Euro 2000 got very excited. But the Toon Army knew it was a non-starter. We read a little further into the interview, where Shearer said, 'I think I have benefited from my decision to retire. I don't miss the criticism, that's for sure.'

He was a better and fitter player for having dedicated himself exclusively to Newcastle United, and those who had forced England's best striker into early International retirement would have to live with their mistake. Sure enough, the next day Shearer issued a statement saying, 'I feel it is only right and fair to make it absolutely clear that I do not wish to be considered for future selection by the England coach.' And you can keep your England shirt.

Our failure to win in Milan had taken some shine off the Barcelona match. Not only did we need to beat the Spaniards at St James', but we had to rely on Inter failing to win in Leverkusen. Few Toon fans expected the German side to hold up their end of the bargain. Nevertheless, the ground was sold out, and 52,000 fans sought to cheer their side to a victory over Barca, even if it would be a last hurrah in the Champions League. Unfortunately, Barca hadn't read the script.

Newcastle dominated for long periods, and Bellamy was incredibly unlucky not to score on several occasions. But, in the second half, Kluivert nipped in to score after hesitation between Bramble and Given. Then Motta volleyed in a Riquelme cross. By this time news had filtered through that Inter were leading in Leverkusen. Inter won 2-0, and United lost 2-0. But Newcastle went out of the Champions League with heads held high.

The Toon Army gave their heroes a standing ovation, and a proud manager and set of players responded in kind. We had done brilliantly to even qualify for the competition, and to progress to the second stage, and then to within a whisker of the quarter-finals, was a fantastic achievement. 'We've enjoyed the ride,' said Bobby. 'We've paid the money, got the ride, got off the tramcar, let's go again.'

Blackburn had put five goals past us to win 5-2 at Ewood Park earlier in the season. Now they visited St James' Park to face a much-improved Newcastle side with that remarkable undefeated post-Champions League record. A vibrant Laurent Robert looked to be the catalyst for victory. Halfway through the opening period, the Frenchman twisted and turned in the box, before lifting a great ball to Nobby Solano, who headed home at the back post.

It was 1-0 at half-time, but the game had been pretty even, and Blackburn equalised 10 minutes into the second half, with Damien Duff's long-range drive across a crowded penalty area. But Robert was very much on his game. First, he forced an astounding save from towering Blackburn goalkeeper Brad Friedel from a top-corner-bound free-kick. Then he curled a second free-kick around the defensive wall and into the bottom corner of the net to restore Newcastle's lead. The score remained 2-1 until the final five minutes.

With a number of spectators inexplicably heading for the exits, Hugo Viana played in Aaron Hughes on the left. Hughesie's cutback found Jermaine Jenas, and the youngster smashed a side-footer into the net. Then Kieron Dyer burst through to the byline, and his driven cross was deflected into his own net by Blackburn defender Gresko. And, in the last minute, Viana's smart cross was knocked in by Craig Bellamy. It finished 5-1, suitably eclipsing Blackburn's 5-2, and the team received a well-deserved ovation from the, admittedly thinned, crowd.

The mystery of fans paying upwards of £25 to watch the match yet leaving before the final whistle was picked up on by Sir Bobby in his post-match interview. 'When will they learn?' he said. 'I feel like saying to them, 'Do you realise what you are watching out there? Don't leave early. It is brilliant stuff.' It's great entertainment, isn't it? We have to get them here early in case Alan Shearer scores in 10 seconds again and make certain they wait for their tea because they might miss another grand finale.'

01 Mar 2003 Premiership	Newcastle United 2 Chelsea 1
05 Mar 2003 Premiership	Middlesbrough 1 Newcastle United 0
11 Mar 2003 Champions League	Inter Milan 2 Newcastle United 2
15 Mar 2003 Premiership	Charlton Athletic 0 Newcastle United 2
19 Mar 2003 Champions League	Newcastle United 0 Barcelona 2
22 Mar 2003 Premiership	Newcastle United 5 Blackburn 1

Premiership: 3rd
Champions League Group A: 3rd – Eliminated

CHAPTER ELEVEN

April

ALONG Strawberry Place behind St James' Gallowgate End, before every home match, stand two female buskers strumming out a succession of pop tunes and terrace anthems in an unrelentingly cheery fashion. They are very enthusiastic, although plainly tone deaf. But they have nothing on legendary Geordie busker Harry Palmer.

The beer-bellied, shades-wearing, guitar-playing troubadour was a regular at Newcastle's away games in the late 1980s and early 1990s, bashing out two-chord monotone versions of Toon anthems, plus a number of his own compositions (to the tune of *Oh When The Saints Go Marching In*: 'Oh when the beans, come out the tin! Oh when the beans come out the tin! I wanna be by that toaster! Oh when the beans come out the tin!').

Harry's fame rocketed during the halcyon days of the Keegan era (to *Yankee Doodle Dandy*: 'Kevin Keegan left the Toon in a helicopter! He came back with Terry Mac and saved us from disaster!'). But tragedy followed. Harry fell down the steps at St James' Park and banged his head, having slipped on a meat pie. He disappeared for several years, before making a welcome, but ultimately ill-fated, comeback appearance during which he was upstaged by Geordie Elvis impersonator Alevis Broon.

Harry's departure left a portly hole in Newcastle's music scene, which could never be filled by the likes of PJ and Duncan, The Lighthouse Family, or even Gazza, with his beer-swilling 'reworking' of *Fog On The Tyne*. And certainly the region's batch of TV talent show popstars fail to match up. When a handbag-carrying Cheryl Tweedy of pop group Girls Aloud high-heeled her way on to the muddy St James' Park pitch to be presented to the crowd during a half-time interval, the embarrassingly thin applause and numerous shrugs and bemused looks said it all.

It would be fair to surmise that Sir Bobby Robson would have been among those who had no idea who Cheryl Tweedy was. During the trip to Barcelona, after being informed that he was staying in the same hotel as popstar Shakira, Bobby commented, 'We have had Shaka Hislop on our books, but I've never heard of Shakira. Is she a singer?'

Newcastle, cultural behemoth, with its glass-fronted bars, pavement cafes, and arts centres, has come a long way, baby. Visitors with false preconceptions of flat caps and whippets now come away suitably corrected. In football terms, the city prospers. But musically, the city is living on scraps. It's a crying shame, because football and music go together like, well, beans and toast. They're passionate, exciting, important things. To coin a local phrase, it's aal wrang.

It was *The Tube*, the only decent programme ever produced by tinpot Tyne Tees Television (and I'm including *Supergran* here), that put Newcastle on the musical map. Every week, the inept and foul-mouthed presenting duo of Paula Yates and Jools Holland brought cutting edge live acts to Newcastle. And the city's late and lamented music venues, the Mayfair and the legendary Riverside, played host to every band who would go on to be anyone.

Not that Newcastle didn't already have a deep-rooted musical heritage. It was, after all, in this city that Eurovision Song Contest popsters Bucks Fizz were involved in a near-fatal bus crash. Also, contrary to popular belief, 1960s beat group The Animals did not have a house in New Orleans. They did, however, have a house in Whitley Bay.

Shadows guitar-twanger Hank Marvin was born and raised in Newcastle, and Mark Knopfler grew up in Gosforth. Sting, then plain old Gordon Sumner, is from Wallsend, and spent years touring Newcastle's working men's clubs. AC/DC frontman Brian Johnson is a Geordie, formerly of Geordie group Geordie. And Chris Rea, although from Middlesbrough, did often deliver ice cream to his uncle's shop in Benwell.

All of these soon-to-be stars buggered off as soon as they had enough money. But Newcastle had its own burgeoning music scene of which to be proud, spearheaded in the 1970s by Lindisfarne (three top 10 hits, so snigger ye not), and in the 1980s by Kitchenware Records, most notably home to Langley Park's Prefab Sprout, but also to Newcastle's The Kane Gane (six chart hits), Martin Stephenson and The Daintees (three chart hits), and, erm, Hurrah (none).

And although Newcastle's football-music interface was irreparably shattered in 1996 by the Toon's horrific Sting-penned Cup Final song, the Geordie legacy of football-friendly music lives on. Harry Palmer still has a place in the tape decks of cars transporting the Toon Army to away matches, as do Lindisfarne, Busker, and, erm, Star Turn On 45 Pints.

I can't count the number of times I've been cheered up on the way back from an away reverse by the sound of Busker's *Home Newcastle*, or Lindisfarne's *Run For Home* playing on the car stereo. Those songs might not trouble critic's choice lists, but, if you're black and white, they mean something. When Cheryl Tweedy records something that makes me feel proud to be a Geordie I'll happily applaud her on to the pitch. Until then I'll await the return of the fat bloke in the sunglasses, and my Harry Palmer tape will stay in the car. 'Oh when the beans, come out the tin…'

Now every game was a cup final. The trip to Everton on 6 April was a great opportunity to close the gap on the two teams above us. With Manchester United set to visit St James' in the following week, the top of the table was tantalisingly close. But Everton had reason of their own to chase the points. They were closing in on a Champions League place, and their rejuvenated side was buoyant. Young Wayne Rooney was fresh from an exciting full

England debut, and the media hyped up the clash between Alan Shearer and Rooney as 'England old' and 'England new'. Within 20 minutes, they got the story they hoped for, when Rooney headed home from close range. Before half-time, a fantastic Jonathan Woodgate long pass found Laurent Robert on the edge of Everton's penalty area, and the Frenchman's rocket of a left-foot shot flew across the goalkeeper into the far corner of the net.

It was 1-1 at half-time and Newcastle looked more than capable of taking the points. But that was reckoning without our refereeing nemesis Neale Barry, the man who had robbed Newcastle of three points against Arsenal by ludicrously sending off Laurent Robert for supposedly delaying a free-kick.

Midway through the second half, Olivier Bernard challenged for a 50-50 ball with Everton's Thomas Graveson, within spitting distance of the referee. Graveson, already booked and lucky to be on the pitch after a succession of bad tackles, clattered high and horrifically into Bernard, ramming his studs into the Frenchman's knee to leave him rolling in agony. The referee took a long look. Graveson immediately gestured for medical attention for Bernard. The referee took a second look. The Newcastle team and bench desperately appealed for a free-kick. The referee waved play on. Everton manager David Moyes and his bench frantically called for his players to put the ball out of play so that Bernard could receive treatment. Both linesmen failed to react. Everton pushed forward. Rooney played the ball to Kevin Campbell. Jonathan Woodgate made a fair challenge in the box. And the referee pointed to the penalty spot. Despite looking at the injured player twice, and in the face of numerous protests from both home and away players and benches, Neale Barry inexplicably let play continue and awarded a penalty to Everton. The Everton players, save for Graveson, were blameless. David Unsworth scored his penalty, and the game ended in a 2-1 defeat. Once again, Neale Barry had derailed Newcastle's title campaign. We were gutted. Lower even than we had been after the Wolves cup defeat. And, surely, there would now be no way back.

'The referee played on when he knew the player was injured,' said Sir

Bobby. 'It was a crucial decision. It cost us the match. It was a massive defeat, and has killed our chances.'

The visit of Manchester United on the following Saturday should have been a tumultuous title clash. But the demise of Newcastle's title hopes, coupled with a 12.30 kick-off, meant some of the gloss had been removed from the fixture by the time the Toon Army made their sober way up to St James'. Still, a win was essential. The title was all but out of reach, but there were still points to be won to secure Champions League qualification. And a victory would severely dent Manchester's chances of winning the title. And that would be nice.

Despite the fervour of the crowd, the game started slowly. Newcastle looked sluggish, yet took the lead against the run of play, when Jermaine Jenas crashed a superb 25-yard volley into the top left-hand corner of the net after 21 minutes. Newcastle had the initiative, but, without the likes of Gary Speed and Laurent Robert, they allowed Manchester to fight back. Within 10 minutes the scores were level when Ole Gunnar Solskjaer beat the offside trap and finished well. Two minutes later, Paul Scholes volleyed home after a neat one-two. Newcastle's fightback had to come now. But it didn't. Within minutes, Scholes eclipsed JJ's effort with an even better 25-yard volley into the top corner of the net. And, just before half-time, John O'Shea's shot rebounded off Newcastle's crossbar to Ryan Giggs, who finished with his right foot.

Newcastle were 4-1 down at half-time, and the Toon Army were shell-shocked. Just 20 minutes earlier the Toon had been in charge, yet now the match seemed to be over. It would take some effort to fight back. But effort was the very thing Newcastle's weary side lacked.

Scholes notched his hat-trick goal after the break, and a Ruud Van Nistelrooy penalty soon followed. It was 6-1 with half an hour still to play. This was unbelievable, embarrassing. Hundreds of disgruntled Newcastle fans headed for the exits.

And then something extraordinary happened. No, Newcastle did not fight back, nor even improve. But the Toon Army, defeated and sore, began to sing, loud and proud, 'We love you Newcastle we do', and 'We'll support you ever more'. It was lump-in-throat stuff, and the debacle on the pitch couldn't spoil it. The fans got some sort of reward when, four minutes from time, substitute Shola Ameobi burst through and chipped the keeper to make it 6-2. And so it ended, still a massive, bruising defeat, but the Toon Army, if not the Toon players, could leave with heads held high.

'We were 6-1 down, and the crowd were magical,' said Sir Bobby Robson after the match.

We headed to the pub to watch Sunderland play Birmingham. If Sunderland lost they would be relegated. But the talk was of Newcastle's misfortune. It was agreed that it was a freak result, brought about by a combination of Newcastle playing terribly and Manchester playing brilliantly. But what a day for such a freak result to occur.

Sunderland did lose to Birmingham, and were relegated. I managed a half-hearted punch in the air. But, like the fans around me, I was too gutted at Newcastle's calamity to celebrate Sunderland's drop into the Nationwide League. It would take a long time to get over this massive defeat. But it wasn't time to throw the rope over the beam quite yet. There were still five matches to play, and Champions League qualification was still very much in our hands.

When you devote so much time to Newcastle United, it's inevitable that other aspects of your life will suffer. In the Toon Army survey, 31 per cent of fans said their support of Newcastle caused conflicts with work, friends, family, and in other relationships.

Jason Hebron from Winlaton occasionally misses work due to Toon Army commitments. 'Because I have a shift system it has always been the case that if there is a midweek fixture or an early kick-off on a Saturday I have to ring in sick.'

Ross Lumsden from Nottingham, by way of Benwell, has pulled many a 'sicky' in order to get to midweek games. And he has experienced conflict with girlfriends and family. 'My girlfriend dumped me because I went to the

1998 cup final instead of her Mam's birthday,' he says. 'And my uncle Billy is a Mackem, so you can imagine the conflict there.'

Spugsy from Newcastle has missed birthdays and holidays, and has 'been on the piss after Toon matches and ended up missing work a few times.'

RK, an exiled Geordie in Japan, says, 'I'm often late for work having listened to the webcast or watched the game at four in the morning. And I've upset my parents on countless occasions, pissing off to the match when they have been planning dinners and the like.'

'New girlfriends take a bit of time to realise how much the team means to me,' says Mark Hadfield from London. 'Also, when considering whether to take a new job money doesn't come into it. It's whether I can get a decent amount of days off to watch the Toon.'

As Newcastle lined up against Fulham at Loftus Road, I sat, along with all of my match-going companions, hundreds of miles away in a pub in Edinburgh. We were here for Pep's long-planned stag night, right in the middle of a crucial and packed fixture period, but arranged to clash with a London away match so as to cause as little disruption to our football viewing as possible. We gathered around a TV showing Sky Soccer Saturday, and Steve pulled up match commentary on his mobile phone. And we began as excruciating a two hours as any football fan could wish to spend.

Five minutes before half-time, Newcastle were ahead, with Alan Shearer heading home a Hugo Viana corner. But, after an hour, the Sky vidiprinter flashed 'Andy Griffin Sent Off – Two Yellow Cards'. United were down to 10 men. From what we could ascertain, Fulham were on top, and a few minutes later, Sylvain Legwinski hit an equaliser from 30 yards. On we held, and we agreed we would now settle for a draw. But, four minutes from time, former Newcastle player and die-hard Toon fan Lee Clark scored Fulham's winner.

We were gutted, and disgruntled. We hadn't been there, so couldn't point fingers, but, if Newcastle had applied themselves, surely they should have overcome lowly Fulham. We trooped back to our hotel disconsolate, got changed, headed back out, and numbed our disappointment with copious amounts of alcohol.

Aston Villa visited St James' on Easter Monday, having done us a big favour. While Newcastle were going down at Fulham, Chelsea were suffering a similar fate at Villa, meaning the Magpies retained their slim Champions League advantage over the Blues. Despite its importance, the match got off to a lethargic start. It was almost half-time before the deadlock was broken. Gareth Barry fouled Kieron Dyer, and then kicked away the ball, allowing ref Jeff Winter to move the free-kick forward 10 yards to the edge of the Villa penalty area. From there, Nobby Solano curled a fantastic right-foot shot over the wall and into the top corner of the net.

Villa fought back, but looked toothless upfront, until the arrival of substitute Dion Dublin. Inexplicably unmarked at a free-kick, Dublin scored with virtually his first touch. The game ended 1-1, Chelsea and Liverpool both won, and Newcastle dropped to fourth in the league, behind the Londoners, clinging on to a Champions League place by fingernails, and with a massive Tyne-Wear derby against Sunderland to follow.

Timed brilliantly to coincide with the build-up to the derby match, the City of Sunderland's hilarious 'Nice one, Sunderland!' local TV ad campaign offered yet another chance to sing 'Let's All Laugh At Sunderland!' Bizarrely soundtracked by the Village People's 1979 gay disco anthem *Go West*, the ad attempted to paint Sunderland as an attractive tourist destination, showcasing such non-attractions as The National Glass Centre and The Bridges shopping centre. In the ad, football, and Sunderland AFC, were conspicuous by their absence.

Despite Sunderland having been relegated two weeks before, with Newcastle's title challenge having effectively expired on the same day, none of the fervour had been removed from the match at the Stadium of Light. Newcastle needed three points in order to remain in contention for a Champions League place, and Sunderland wanted to take at least some pride from an awful season. This would be the last Tyne-Wear derby for some time, and the loser would have to endure a long wait before they would have the opportunity to take revenge.

Although fans can never properly look forward to a derby match because the consequences of losing are so great, the pubs around St James' Park on the sunny morning of the match were full of grinning Geordies, confidently predicting a famous victory. 'I'm worried because I'm not worried,' said Steve, as he headed to Ladbrokes to back a 3-1 Toon win.

45 free coaches had been provided to transport Mags the short distance from St James' to the Stadium of Light, and the convoy was greeted with waves and toots from passing motorists, and passed various specially altered road signs (including, of course, 'Stadium of Shite') during the short but slow journey south. Several coaches stopped at the roadside so inebriated fans could relieve themselves on the grass verges, and big Beefy pressed his NUFC belly tattoo against a bus window to cheers from passing fans.

As the Toon Army entered Sunderland, the expected army of red and white hordes hurling abuse and volleys of half-bricks failed to materialise. Inside the ground, there was a scrum for the bar, and the singing began in earnest. A Newcastle fanzine had printed up thousands of black and white banners reading, 'LET'S ALL LAUGH AT SUNDERLAND! HA HA!' Geordies held aloft and rattled keys in reference to the Mackems' strange pronunciation ('Weys keys are theys keys?'). Passports were waved, mocking Sunderland's lack of European experience, and the favourite song from Newcastle's exciting Champions League campaign was resurrected: 'Have you ever seen a Mackem in Milan?'

As the kick-off approached, Sunderland fans were serenaded with Vera Lynn's *We'll Meet Again*, and, with reference to the departed Peter Reid, 'You should have stuck with the monkey'. Incredibly, as the game began, there were hundreds of empty seats around the stadium. 'You couldn't sell all your tickets,' we sang.

Within seconds of the start, a heavily-bandaged Alan Shearer had the ball in the back of the Sunderland net, but the goal was disallowed for a push. Newcastle's Shay Given was forced to make a couple of smart saves, but Thomas Sorensen was the busiest of the goalkeepers, saving several times from Craig Bellamy.

Despite losing Alan Shearer to injury, Newcastle's superior pace and skill eventually paid dividends. Bellamy burst into the penalty area and was clattered by Kevin Kilbane. It was the clearest penalty imaginable, but, inevitably, 40,000 Mackems disagreed. Nobby Solano ably deputised for Shearer, sending Sorensen the wrong way from the spot. One-nil, and the Toon Army exploded with delight and relief.

Newcastle held on through the second half until, deep into injury time, Kevin Kyle rose to head the ball into Shay Given's net. Scores of home fans excitedly jumped barriers to goad the Toon Army, despite the fact that referee Steve Bennett had correctly signalled a free-kick for a foul on Given. The goal was disallowed, and the game ended 1-0 to Newcastle.

'You're just the worst team in history,' sang the Toon Army, as the Stadium of Light emptied. By the time we were allowed to leave the ground, the defeated Mackems had beaten a hasty retreat, leaving just three schoolboys, sipping illegally-procured cans of lager in a bush, to half-heartedly flick V-signs at the departing coaches. In the stadium car park, Sunderland's Kevin Kyle was so distracted by the baying Toon Army that he was almost run over by a car.

So the Toon Army, and Tyne-Wear bragging rights, returned to Newcastle, leaving a famous valediction ringing around Wearside: 'We'll meet again, Don't know where, Don't know when, But I know we'll meet again some sunny day...'

06 Apr 2003 Premiership	Everton 2 Newcastle United 1
12 Apr 2003 Premiership	Newcastle United 2 Manchester United 6
19 Apr 2003 Premiership	Fulham 2 Newcastle United 1
21 Apr 2003 Premiership	Newcastle United 1 Aston Villa 1
26 Apr 2003 Premiership	Sunderland 0 Newcastle United 1

Premiership: 3rd

CHAPTER TWELVE

May

WE sat in the sun sipping cool pints before the last home game of the season. With two league games left to play, we stood third in the Premiership table, one point ahead of both Chelsea and Liverpool. The top four sides would go into the Champions League. A maximum six points from our two remaining matches would ensure Champions League football returned to Tyneside.

Birmingham City were today's visitors, a nondescript side that had already guaranteed their Premiership survival. Most of the pre-match talk was of our Champions League chances. Even without Alan Shearer, a sprained ankle (coupled with a split head and a broken wrist) having finally put an end to his season, we reckoned this looked to be a straightforward victory.

As we headed up to St James', we passed signs saying, 'You are now entering an area where commercial filming is taking place. If you do not consent to being filmed, please avoid the area.' 52,000 Geordies had little choice but to consent to being filmed. As it was, it appeared the cameras were more interested in groups of extras wearing fake sponsor-free black and white shirts. We headed past the buskers, up to Leazes terrace, and into our seats for the final time before summer intervened.

Newcastle were by far the better of the two teams, but poor finishing kept the scores level until the 40th minute. Craig Bellamy burst through the Birmingham defence, and was barged over by Mathew Upson. David Elleray, refereeing his last match before retirement, saw Upson as the last defender and showed him the red card. From the free-kick, 20 yards out, and in the absence of Laurent Robert, Hugo Viana curled a perfect shot over the wall and into the top corner of the net.

At half-time, former Toon striker Mickey Quinn took to the pitch, receiving one of the best receptions yet for a returning hero. The Mighty Quinn scored 63 goals in 126 appearances for Newcastle during the late 1980s and early 1990s. His goals were the highlight of an underachieving period, and the stocky horse-racing fanatic became a legend during that time.

In the second half, Kieron Dyer hit the post and Shola Ameobi hit the crossbar, but the score remained 1-0. As the final whistle blew, attention turned elsewhere. Latest scores had both Chelsea and Liverpool drawing their respective games. But there were developments as the matches reached their conclusion. First, Paulo Di Canio came off the bench to score a winner for West Ham against Chelsea. Then, deep into injury time, former Liverpool player Nicolas Anelka scored a winner for Manchester City against Liverpool. Newcastle had won, Chelsea and Liverpool had lost. Newcastle were now four points ahead of both sides, with only one game to play. Newcastle were guaranteed third place in the Premiership, and Champions League football in 2003-2004.

'Geordies in the Champions League!' rang out across St James' Park, as Newcastle United's players and staff gathered on the pitch for a lap of honour. Bobby Robson furiously beckoned toward the tunnel, and, eventually, a cast-wearing Alan Shearer hobbled on to the pitch. 'Shearer! Shearer!' The squad made their way around the pitch, applauding and taking applause. Sir Bobby Robson, fists clenched in celebration, seemed to be trying to make eye contact with every supporter in the stadium, thanking them individually for their support. As he looked at me, he appeared to mouth the words, 'Next year'. A lump the size of a football formed in my throat. The Toon Army returned their thanks. 'There's only one Bobby Robson! One Bobby Robson! Walking along, singing a song! Walking in a Robson wonderland!'

Back at the pub, I bought a pint and grinned as I looked at the league table on the TV sets around me. Steve arrived, whistling and skipping like a character in an MGM musical. At one point I swear he leapt into the air and clicked his heels. As Dave and the rest of the lads arrived, we shook hands and celebrated.

'Bad news. Looks like we'll be spending more long nights in exotic foreign climes, supping strangely-named European lagers next season!'

'Geddin!'

On the following day, Arsenal lost to Leeds at Highbury, handing the Premiership to Manchester United. It was no disgrace for us to come third behind Man United and Arsenal. Both of those teams had been better than us over the course of the season. But we thoroughly deserved our third place, having been superior to both Chelsea and Liverpool. With improvements over the summer, there was no reason why we couldn't close the gap on Man United and Arsenal and actually win some silverware.

'Newcastle is a brilliant, manic football city,' said Kieron Dyer, Newcastle's stand-in skipper in the absence of Alan Shearer. 'Yet you get the feeling the supporters have become used to the team falling short, whether it is in the league or in the cups. We have to change that mentality around the place. Any silverware, whatever it might be, would be a sign we are going places. We need something to show for our efforts and offer the supporters.'

Again, I thought of Sir Bobby: 'Next year…'

Newcastle had worn their new home shirt for the first time in the match against Birmingham. Designed by Adidas, the opinion in the pub after the game was that it was 'too white'. With white shoulders and arms, it looked more like a St Mirren shirt than a Newcastle United one.

'We're meant to play in black and white stripes, not in white with black stripes,' was one slightly confusing comment. Despite our misgivings, we would all be buying the shirt, and proudly wearing it come the new season.

Newcastle teacher George Stainsby prefers his old 1979 Bukta replica shirt. 'My two best ideas this year have involved football,' he says. 'One involved a bunch of 11-year olds-writing their own commentary on Liam O'Brien's free-kick against the Mackems in 1992. The other was an assignment about advertising that included the kids designing an advert to sell a Toon strip to the same loons. During the assignment I hung up my old Bukta shirt on the board. Jamie, a 14-year-old football obsessive, did a quick David Dickinson: "Eh, sir, did the Toon really wear a top like that? The badge is funny! You should sell it and make a fortune!" "I don't think it's worth much, Jamie," I replied. Except, of course, I do know how much it's worth. Everything.'

Internet auction site eBay regularly does a roaring trade in vintage Newcastle United shirts. On one particular day there were 202 different Newcastle tops for sale on the site, ranging from 99p for a child's grubby 1995 home shirt to £295 for a signed Alan Shearer 2002 away shirt. Also available were various away shirts (in denim blue, royal blue, green, yellow, all black, all white, claret and blue hoops...), a classic Umbro 1980s home shirt for a fiver, plus the brand new home shirt, despite the fact that it had yet to be officially released.

The new Adidas shirt bore the logo of the club's new main sponsor, Northern Rock. This caused consternation on Wearside. In 1996, Sunderland fans refused to buy Sugar Puffs after the cereal makers chose Kevin Keegan to front a TV ad campaign. Newcastle fans stopped drinking PG Tips during Peter Reid's Sunderland reign for a similar reason. And Black Cats fans were now boycotting Northern Rock because the building society had placed its name on the shirts of their deadly rivals. Apparently, Sunderland fans were going to be putting their money into the Nationwide...

Meanwhile, the spectre of the 'Superfan' was once again raised, this time by Tony Blair's favourite website, the very poor official Newcastle United club site. It launched a 'competition to find the club's most LOYAL and

UNIQUE fan'. The shortlist included someone who lives in Kent, a lady who prefers NUFC socks to lingerie, a 'southern-based fan', a woman who has had her nose broken twice at St James' Park, someone with a dog named 'Keegan', someone with a dog called 'Sir Bobby', and the St James' Park tea-lady, 'much respected by the local and national press', who has never seen a match because she is always working. The website charged a hefty £34.99 for a 12-month subscription, but its competition was as cheap as chips.

The final match of the season, before the onset of another lonely summer, took us via the A1, the M6, and Spaghetti Junction, to the Hawthorns and West Bromwich Albion. Despite showing tremendous fighting spirit, West Brom's cut-price side had already been relegated, although admittedly not quite in the same record-breaking style as Sunderland. During their visit to Newcastle earlier in the season, they had been narrowly beaten 2-1, and their fans had shown themselves to be the noisiest set of away supporters St James' Park had seen over the season. With the 'Boing-Boing Baggies' bidding a fond farewell to the Premiership, and the Toon Army celebrating Champions League qualification, it promised to be a carnival affair.

From newspaper and radio coverage it became apparent that all eyes would be elsewhere today. Bolton Wanderers needed to better West Ham's result as the pair battled relegation, Chelsea and Liverpool were fighting for the final Champions League spot. We couldn't decide on which team we wanted to go down or which team we wanted to get into the Champions League. This isn't an unusual occurrence when you want every team apart from your own to lose every game they are involved in, even though, by the very nature of the game of football, this can't possibly happen. We couldn't decide whether we wanted Arsenal or Southampton to win the following week's FA Cup Final, either. Usually we'd side with the underdogs – Southampton, in this case. But a Southampton victory would mean that club had won two major trophies in the time since Newcastle last won anything. And we couldn't have Southampton running away from us in the success stakes. So the rest of football's gaze was averted, drawn to more important events elsewhere, but we arrived in West Bromwich determined to enjoy ourselves, and send our team into the summer break with a pat on the back for a season well done. After our last pre-match pints of the season, and having set down yet more cash at Ladbrokes, we took our places.

In the absence of Alan Shearer, stand-in Shola Ameobi's name was announced over the tannoy as 'Shola Amoeba'. 'One cell! He's only got one cell!' With the likes of Woodgate, Bellamy, and Robert also unavailable, there were opportunities for younger players, including places on the bench for Michael Chopra and new signing from Nottingham Forest Darren Ambrose. But the depleted side struggled against the tenacious Baggies.

Midway through the first half, the West Brom supporters said farewell to their cult hero Bob Taylor, playing his last competitive match. The Toon Army offered applause as the injured striker limped from the field. And that typified the good-natured support, with a mutual appreciation society forming between West Brom's Baggies and Newcastle's Toon Army.

It was the Toon Army who were first to celebrate a goal. Jermaine Jenas capped a fine season by rising highest to head home from a corner. '1-0 to the Premier League!' sang the Toon Army. And, for the first time all season, and in the very last match, we won a first goalscorer bet. Who said we wouldn't win anything this season? It wasn't quite the championship, but, at 14 to 1, it couldn't be sniffed at. Courtesy of another bet, a 4-1 Newcastle victory would increase our winning odds to 264 to 1. West Brom scored the '1' shortly after half-time, with Scott Dobie shooting across Shay Given. And our dreams of mega winnings were scuppered when Dobie grabbed a second to give West Brom a 2-1 lead 10 minutes later. '2-1 to the Nationwide!' responded the Baggies. But a West Brom victory would have been unfair on such an even-handed day. When a shirtless West Brom fan with a tiny child on his shoulders ran on to the pitch, such was the occasion that play continued, and the chap was ushered back into the stand without so much as a slap on the wrist. Parity was ensured when Hugo Viana curled in almost a carbon copy of his free-kick against Birmingham in the previous week.

A draw was an acceptable result on the day, and Newcastle's subdued team deserved no more. The attitude of the team was disappointing at the end of such an enjoyable season, particularly with such magnificent support cheering them on. The players were nevertheless applauded from the pitch, with some, but not all, coming over to return the compliment to the fans. As the West Brom fans stayed behind to cheer their players on a lap of honour, we headed for the exits, clapping the Baggies fans as we went, and offering them a rendition of '*We'll Meet Again*', in more sympathetic style than on our recent visit to Sunderland. As we left the ground, the Newcastle squad were already boarding their bus, having barely had time to have a shower, apparently hurrying back to Newcastle for a boozy night out centring around a Justin Timberlake teen-pop concert. We shook hands with West Brom fans on our way to the car, and then headed home.

Radio reports revealed that Chelsea had beaten Liverpool 2-1 and would join Newcastle in the Champions League. Bolton drew and West Ham lost, meaning the Hammers would be relegated alongside West Brom and Sunderland. After a long drive North, we arrived back in Newcastle.

'What are we going to do with our weekends now?' I asked. No one had an answer.

Newcastle finished the season 2002-03 third in the Premiership with 69 points, 14 points behind Champions Manchester United, and 9 points behind runners-up Arsenal.

Aside from the prize of Champions League qualification, despite failing to win any silverware, Newcastle's season wasn't entirely accolade-free. The Professional Footballers' Association named Alan Shearer the Premier League Overall Player of the Decade. The Toon skipper was also named in the PFA's Premiership Team of the Season alongside Kieron Dyer. Shearer also picked up the North East Footballer of the Year award, and the award for North East Goal of the Season, for his wonder strike against Everton. Most impressively, Jermaine Jenas was named the PFA Young Player of the Year, as well as the North East Young Player of the Year. Individual gongs are something for players rather than fans to get excited about, but the continuing form of our hero Shearer, coupled with the brilliant ability of young players like Jenas, pointed to exciting times around the corner.

'Although it has been a good season, we all feel it could have been a little bit better,' reflected Alan Shearer, speaking on BBC Radio Newcastle. 'I want to win something. I've been here seven years. One of the reasons I came back here was to win silverware. We've been so near but yet so far. I want to win something for Bobby Robson, I want to win something for myself, and I want to win something for the fans. I've come home from Wembley on two occasions when we've been losers, and the turn out for the parade the following day has just been unbelievable for a team that's been beaten. I want to be part of a team that wins because I want to see the celebrations when we do actually bring a piece of silverware home.'

Meanwhile, Sunderland ended the season with a 3-0 home defeat courtesy of Arsenal. The Black Cats finished rock bottom of the Premiership. They managed to break several Premiership records along the way, including the lowest points total (19 out of the available 114), the least goals scored (21 – Newcastle's Alan Shearer scored 25 goals on his own in all competitions), the least wins (4 – 17 victories less than Newcastle), and the most consecutive losses (15 – English football record is 18, set by Darwen in 1899). In addition, the Sunderland club shop in the MetroCentre closed due to financial difficulties. The shop stood on the first floor of the shopping complex, with Newcastle's club shop downstairs, meaning it had been the only instance in recent memory in which Sunderland had found itself above Newcastle.

So Newcastle United didn't win anything in season 2002-03. No change there. But no Toon fan could feel short-changed. It was the quintessential Newcastle United season – an emotional roller coaster ride of highs and lows.

The jump from the previous season's fourth place to third in the Premiership was a massive achievement. And the Champions League campaign established the club as one of the top 16 sides in Europe, standing on merit alongside Real, Juventus, Milan and all. The domestic cup challenges were the only real failures of the season. The pathetic defeat at Wolves was a real low-point, and one of the few occasions where the players really let us down.

The highlight of the season on the pitch was certainly the victory in Feyenoord. Three thousand Toon fans roared the team on as Bellamy, and Viana, and Bellamy again with his amazing last-gasp winner, scored to send Newcastle into the last 16, despite the fact that we had lost our first three games. UEFA didn't give us a tin cup, but we did get an estimated £10 million, which is canny consolation. Football's biggest club competition also gave us the opportunity for memorable trips to the likes of Juventus, Barcelona, and Inter Milan. And, although we only picked up one point in those three games, they were fantastic trips. This was football at a whole new level.

Looking back, my strongest abiding memory from season 2002-03 is standing in the San Siro in Milan at half-time in the Champions League match, eating a Cornetto under a scoreboard reading 'Inter 0 Newcastle 1'. 'One-nil in the San Siro!' It was so brilliant, so bizarre, so Newcastle United.

And then the summer started, and I thought about going on holiday (I'd need to buy the new Toon shirt), and I drove to Scotland for Pep's wedding (necessarily arranged in the close season), and I read the papers every day for transfer speculation (Bowyer, Beattie, Emerton, Kleberson, Bridges, Bridge… Who would sign, and how much did the club have in its coffers?). The new football season began on 12 August with the Champions League Qualifiers. That was eight weeks away. It would be difficult, but I reckoned I could just about wait it out until the game that means so much to so many rolled around again.

'Supporting Newcastle United means a hell of a lot,' says Razz from Karachi in Pakistan. 'I can't describe it. I just can't imagine me life without the Toon.'

'It gets you out of bed to work jobs we normally hate just to give you the means to follow the Toon,' says Steve Kennedy from Walker.

'It's in the blood,' says Michael Baker from Gosforth. 'I've had some great times, and some not so great, but I love the Toon to death.'

Craig Tither from Gateshead agrees. 'It means everything. It's in the blood. A way of life. Enjoying a couple of pints with the lads before a match, listening to the Geordie humour, the special atmosphere of St James' Park, going through all the emotions when watching the Toon. It's the best. We are the best!'

Lee Shearer from Newcastle says, 'It's more important than life itself. Take NUFC away and what are you left with? Beer.'

'Life with the Toon is a roller coaster of emotions,' says Anth Nicholson from North Shields. 'Winning is important, yet, in my lifetime, there has been little achieved. But this does not detract from the thrill of following the black and whites. Relegations, promotions, various managers, loads of players, and one great consistency – the massive fanatical support of Newcastle United, the only club that matters.'

Jason Hebron from Winlaton says supporting Newcastle means, 'passion, frustration, excitement, goals, the need for and dream of success, but above all loyalty to the best club and best city, while getting the feeling every time I am at the match that this is where I belong.'

'It means everything,' says Warwick Armstrong from Gateshead, 'and I am proud to have two sons who are as Newcastle daft as I am.'

David, exiled 'down south', says, 'Living down south now, I am very proud of where I come from, and I get most of that pride from the Toon. To be honest, I don't really give a toss that we've won nowt in my lifetime. I'd hate to be a Manchester United fan, where the predictability would bore me. The Toon offers a sense of belonging and a means to get hammered every other week!'

Mike Mullins in Austria says, 'I really like the romance of following the Toon. And the good times are going to be amazing once they start!'

'I'm glad that we're now seeing decent football over a sustained period, but I'm frustrated that we're not winning anything,' says Tadger from Rowlands Gill. 'At the start of the Keegan era we were all looking toward the championship, but now I'd settle for the League Cup just to get the ball rolling. I'm glad we're not a sleeping giant anymore, but I'm still clamming for a bit of silverware.'

'We may not win anything,' says Adam Bell from Whickham, ' but it's a good ride all the way.'

Graeme Crisp from Morpeth says, 'I've had a season ticket for 20-odd years and have been going to matches since I was six, so supporting Newcastle is a way of life to me. It's very hard to describe what it means to me, but I'm so proud to be a Newcastle United fan.'

'It means everything,' says Ross Lumsden in Nottingham. 'It's the one thing me and my Dad used to do together when I was a kid, and we still go together to most of the home and away matches now. It's like a family ritual, with me, my Dad, wor kid, and my uncle David. I've been going for 15 years. Here's to another 50. Toon Army 'til I die.'

'I remain confident that our day will come,' says Jamie Smith from Newcastle. 'It's never dull supporting Newcastle, but it's about time we won something. Surely Sir Bobby Robson deserves it, the greatest English centre-forward of our age deserves it, and, damn it, we deserve it. Next year. Up the Mags!'

We are the Toon Army, and Newcastle United permeates every aspect of our lives. For us, football is so much more than a game. It's about roots and family and growing up and finding an identity in the world. It's a source of great joy and no little consternation. It's about having a drink and a laugh with friends. It's a source of release and a brilliant pastime. It's an important and life-affirming thing. It's a part of us and it will be until the day we die.

Ultimately, Bill Shankly was wrong. Football isn't more important than life or death. But it runs them pretty close. Haway the lads.

06 May 2003 Premiership Newcastle United 1 Birmingham 0
11 May 2003 Premiership West Bromwich Albion 2 Newcastle United 2

Premiership: Final Placing 3rd
Champions League: Entry to third qualifying round

Appendix

Toon Army Survey Results

The Toon Army Survey was conducted between October and December 2002. Responses were collected via the website www.toonarmybook.com.

100% of respondents were NUFC supporters.
61% of respondents were NUFC season ticket holders.
23% of respondents were NUFC away match regulars.

Why do you support Newcastle United?

Local team	67%
Family ties	24%
Recent success	1%
Other	8%

Which of the following best describes you?

Local Geordie	50%
Exiled Geordie	33%
Adopted Geordie	15%
Non Geordie	2%

How much do you spend on NUFC in a season, tickets, travel, TV etc?

£0	5%
£500	32%
£750	12%
£1,000	21%

£1,500	10%
£2,000	17%
Over £2,000	3%

How far do you travel to watch NUFC in a season, home and away?

0 miles	12%
100 miles	19%
500 miles	22%
1,000 miles	14%
2,000 miles	21%
Over 2,000 miles	12%

What do you think of Sunderland?

Hate	33%
Dislike	18%
Laugh at	43%
No opinion	6%
Support all local teams	0%

Which of the following would you rather see?

England win the World Cup	10%
Newcastle win FA Cup	90%

Has your support of Newcastle United ever conflicted with the following?

Work	40%
Friends	23%
Family	35%
Other relationships	26%

Who is the best player you've ever seen in a Newcastle shirt?

Peter Beardsley	50%
Alan Shearer	27%

Malcolm Macdonald	6%
Kevin Keegan	5%
Paul Gascoigne	4%
Others	8%

Others polling more than 1 vote: Faustino Asprilla, Kieron Dyer, David Ginola, Robert Lee

And the worst player?

Fumaca	19%
Marcelino	10%
Silvio Maric	8%
Mike Hooper	8%
Rob MacDonald	6%
Frank Pingel	6%
Others	43%

Others polling more than 1 vote: Billy Askew, Kevin Dillon, Wayne Fereday, Des Hamilton, Glen Keeley, Paul Kitson

What is the best moment you've had supporting the Toon?

Promotion to the Premier League 1993	21%
Beating Barcelona in the Champions League 1997	15%
Beating Manchester United 5-0 in Premier League 1996	13%
Beating Feyenoord to qualify for Champions League Second Group Stage 2002	11%
Rob Lee's goal in Wembley FA Cup semi-final versus Chelsea, 2000	9%
Consecutive FA Cup semi-final wins versus Sheffield United and Tottenham1998 and 1999	6%
David Kelly's goal in Second Division survival match versus Portsmouth 1992	4%
European Fairs Cup win versus Ujpesti Doza 1969	4%
Qualifying for the Champions League 1997 and 2002	4%
Others	13%

APPENDIX

And the worst moment?

Consecutive FA Cup Final defeats versus Arsenal and Manchester United 1998 & 1999	21%
Losing to Sunderland at St James' Park in a torrential rainstorm 1999	21%
Losing to Sunderland at St James' Park in First Division play-off 1990	19%
Losing to Chelsea in Wembley FA Cup semi-final 2000	15%
Blowing a 12-point lead to lose the Premier League to Manchester United 1996	11%
Kevin Keegan resignation 1997	6%
FA Cup Final defeat to Liverpool 1974	4%
FA Cup third round replay defeat to Hereford 1972	2%
Others	1%

Index

AEK Athens 40
Almeyda, Matias 74
Ameobi, Shola 20, 53, 66, 79, 84, 113, 115, 136, 142, 146
Anelka, Nicolas 142
Ardiles, Ossie 35
Arsenal 24, 29, 32, 37, 40, 45, 50-1, 68, 75, 95, 97-8, 103, 105-9, 111-12, 116, 134, 143, 145, 147-8, 155
Askew, Billy 46, 154
Asprilla, Faustino 12, 20, 22, 26, 36, 46, 105, 154
Aston Villa 14, 80, 85, 89, 138, 140
Babic, Marko 115
Balis, Igor 56-7
Barcelona 7, 20, 22-3, 27-8, 39-40, 70-1, 81-2, 84-5, 89, 114, 116, 125, 129-30, 132, 149, 154
Barnes, John 23
Barry, Gareth 138
Barry, Neale 108-9, 112, 134
Barthez, Fabien 72
Bartlett, Shaun 62
Barton, Warren 26
Basturk, Yildiray 115
Bayer Leverkusen 70-1, 112-13, 115-16, 125, 129
Bayern Munich 40
Beardsley, Peter 14, 44-5, 97, 99, 153
Beattie, James 71, 149
Beckham, David 16, 72
Bellamy, Craig 19, 33, 43, 52-3, 62, 69, 73-4, 79-81, 85, 88-9, 92, 96-8, 100, 105, 108-9, 112, 123-5, 128-30, 139-40, 142, 146, 149
Benfica 49
Bennett, Steve 140
Bergkamp, Dennis 106, 108-9, 112
Bernard, Olivier 20, 72, 107, 118, 134
Bettega, Roberto 70
Birmingham City 53-4, 141
Blackburn Rovers 36, 57, 59-61, 63, 96, 129-30
Bolton Wanderers 89, 101, 145
Bombarda, Mariano 69
Bowyer, Lee 96, 99
Bramble, Titus 10, 27, 43, 60, 62, 72, 98, 106, 115, 124
Brighton and Hove Albion 35, 44
Buffon, Gianluigi 62
Butt, Nicky 72
Caldwell, Steve 20, 66-7, 72, 98, 115
Cambridge United 56
Campbell, Kevin 67, 79, 106-7, 134
Campbell, Sol 106
Cannavaro, Fabio 74
Cantona, Eric 21, 110
Celtic 34, 126
Champions League 7, 20, 22-3, 26, 29, 34, 39-41, 48-9, 51-4, 56, 61-3, 68-70, 74-5, 81, 89, 93-4, 99, 101, 112-13, 115-16, 121-2, 124, 129-30, 133, 135-6, 138-9, 141-2, 145, 147-9, 151, 154
Charlton, Jack 45
Charlton Athletic 63, 130
Chelsea 22, 24, 34, 45, 48, 53, 97-9, 110, 117-18, 130, 138, 141-3, 145, 147, 154-5
Chopra, Michael 20, 67, 100, 146
Clark, Lee 137
Cole, Andy 21, 36, 44
Cole, Ashley 107
Cole, Joe 96
Cologne 112

INDEX

Conceicao, Sergio 124
Cordoba 124
Cort, Carl 67
Cottbus 113
Cotterill, Steve 57
Coventry City 93
Crespo, Hernan 74
Cruyff, Johann 22
Cudicini, Carlo 118
Cunningham, Tony 45
Dabizas, Nicos 27, 38, 43, 53, 56, 60, 69, 74, 89
Dalglish, Kenny 22, 111
Davids, Edgar 55
Defoe, Jermaine 96
Del Piero, Allesandro 56
Di Canio, Paulo 142
Dillon, Kevin 46, 154
Diouf, El Hadji 126
Distin, Sylvain 97
Dobie, Scott 146
Dublin, Dion 138
Duff, Damien 129
Dunn, David 60
Durham County Cricket Club 126
Dyer, Kieron 10-11, 19, 30, 38-9, 48, 52, 56, 67, 69, 84, 91, 100, 105, 107, 115, 127, 130, 138, 142-3, 147, 154
Dynamo Kiev 40, 48, 53, 63, 68, 74
Elleray, David 142
Emerton, Brett 149
Enrique, Luis 20, 27
Eriksson, Sven Goran 107
European Cup 68, 114
European Fairs Cup 18, 20, 22, 51, 94, 154
Everton 50, 67, 75, 79-80, 89, 97, 133-4, 140, 147
FA Cup 7, 11, 13, 18, 22, 24-5, 42, 71, 78, 89, 92-3, 101, 110-11, 113, 145, 153-5
FC Basle 40
FC Internazionale Milano 121
Ferdinand, Les 21, 89
Ferdinand, Rio 10, 72, 99
Fereday, Wayne 46, 154
Ferguson, Duncan 24
Ferguson, Sir Alex 72
Feyenoord 40-41, 53, 63, 68-9, 74-5, 149, 154
Figo, Luis 20
Fowler, Robbie 99
Friedel, Brad 130
Fulham 85, 89, 113, 118, 120, 137-8, 140
Fumaca, Jose Antunes 46-7, 154
Gabbiadini, Marco 110
Gardner, Ricardo 88
Gascoigne, Paul 44-45, 99, 154
Gates, Eric 110
Geremi 119
Giggs, Ryan 72, 135
Gillespie, Keith 60
Ginola, David 21, 36, 46, 154
Given, Shay 19, 38, 43, 56, 59, 69, 79, 84, 92, 107, 113, 115, 118, 123, 139-40, 146
Goddard, Paul 14
Goma, Alain 85
Graveson, Thomas 134
Gresko, Vratislav 130
Griffin, Andy 20, 53, 60, 62, 80, 84, 137
Grimsby Town 59
Gudjohnsen, Eidur 48
Gullit, Ruud 23-4, 50, 91, 111
Hamilton, Des 23, 46, 154
Hamman, Dietmar 43
Harper, Steve 67
Hartlepool United 103
Hasselbaink, Jimmy Floyd 118
Henry, Thierry 106
Hereford United 25, 42, 110, 155

Higuita, Rene 86
Hislop, Shaka 35, 132
Hoddle, Glenn 88-9, 98
Hooper, Mike 46-7, 154
Howey, Steve 97
Huckerby, Darren 38
Hughes, Aaron 20, 71, 73, 98, 108, 130
Hypia, Sami 43
Ince, Paul 92
Inter Milan 40, 70, 74-5, 112, 121, 130, 149
Ipswich Town 93, 113
James, David 33, 96
Jenas, Jermaine 20, 34, 43, 62, 92, 96-8, 100, 107, 113, 119, 130, 135, 146-8
Juventus 40, 54-6, 62-3, 68-70, 148-9
Keane, Robbie 98-9
Keane, Roy 64, 72
Keegan, Kevin 13-14, 20, 24-5, 34-7, 44-5, 47, 72, 78, 97, 99, 111, 131, 144-5, 150, 154-5
Keeley, Glen 46, 154
Keller, Kasey 98
Kelly, David 21-2, 36, 109, 154
Kennedy, Mark 92
Ketsbaia, Temuri 23, 127
Kewell, Harry 48
Khatskevitch, Alexander 49
Kilbane, Kevin 140
Kitson, Paul 46, 154
Kleberson 149
Kluivert, Patrick 27, 84, 129
Kyle, Kevin 140
Lampard, Frank 118
Lee, Rob 21-2, 24, 36, 110, 154
Leeds United 48, 53, 96, 114, 116
Legwinski, Sylvain 137
Leicester City 21, 36
Lineker, Gary 44
Liverpool 25, 29, 40, 42-4, 47, 50, 53, 59, 90, 101, 126, 138, 141-3, 145, 147, 155
Lua Lua, Lomana 20, 31, 33, 91, 112-13, 124
Lurling, Anthony 69
Luton Town 45
Macdonald, Malcolm 44, 74, 154
MacDonald, Rob 46-7, 154
Manchester City 34, 37, 41, 50, 97, 99, 101, 106, 142
Manchester United 7, 11, 14, 16, 21, 24-5, 29, 32, 34-6, 40, 50-1, 64, 71-3, 75, 78, 87, 97-8, 103, 106, 110-12, 118, 133, 135, 140, 143, 147, 150, 154-5
Maradona, Diego 22
Marcelino, Elena 46-7, 154
Maric, Silvio 46, 154
Marsden, Chris 85
Materazzi, Marco 74
McCarthy, Mick 121
McClaren, Steve 66
McGhee, Mark 110
Middlesbrough 103
Motta, Thago 84, 129
Moyes, David 134
Murphy, Danny 57
Murray, Bob 57
Nadal, Jordina 20
Nash, Carlo 97
Nationwide League 38, 136
Ndah, George 92
Nesta, Alessandro 10
Neuville, Oliver 115
NK Zeljeznicar 29-30, 39, 41
Norman, Tony 110
Norwich City 93
Nottingham Forest 28, 93, 146
O'Shea, John 135
O'Brien, Andy 20, 53, 56, 89, 95, 106, 115, 117
O'Brien, Liam 144
Okocha, Jay Jay 88

INDEX

Overmars, Marc 84
Owen, Michael 43
Oxford United 35, 80, 93
Palmer, Harry 131, 133
Pardo, Sebastian 53
Peacock, Darren 21
Peacock, Gavin 36
Pingel, Frank 46-7, 154
Pires, Robert 107
Pistone, Alessandro 67
Portsmouth 22, 36, 109, 154
Poyet, Gus 98, 110-11
Professional Footballers' Association 147
PSV Eindhoven 114
Quinn, Mickey 142
Radford, Ronnie 42, 92, 110
Real Madrid 40, 111
Reid, Peter 12, 52, 57, 139, 144
Reilly, George 47
Rennie, Uriah 38, 88, 96
Ricketts, Michael 88
Ridsdale, Peter 99, 114
Riquelme, Juan Roman 129
Rivaldo 10-11, 20
Robert, Laurent 7, 19, 43, 53, 56, 60, 62, 67, 72, 79, 90, 99, 107, 111, 117, 124, 127, 129, 134-5, 142
Robinson, Paul 48
Robson, Sir Bobby 7, 10, 19, 33-4, 37, 42, 62, 67, 72, 74, 89-90, 95, 98, 103, 105, 111, 113-14, 126, 128, 132, 136, 142-3, 148, 151
Roeder, Glenn 14, 33
Roma 40
Romario 127
Ronaldinho 11
Ronaldo 10, 22
Rooney, Wayne 79, 133-4
Scholes, Paul 72, 112, 135
Seaman, David 11, 107-9
Shankly, Bill 151
Shatskikh, Maxim 49, 63
Shearer, Alan 16, 19, 23, 27, 31, 33, 36, 38-9, 43-4, 52, 56, 58, 60-1, 63, 72-4, 79-80, 85, 91-3, 96-7, 99-100, 106, 115, 123-5, 127-8, 130, 134, 137, 139, 141-4, 146-8, 153
Sheffield United 22, 154
Shepherd, Freddy 99, 126
Shoulder, Alan 16
Singh, Harpal 100
Smith, Alan 48, 114
Solano, Nolberto 'Nobby' 19, 33-4, 43, 53, 57, 60, 63, 74, 84-5, 88-9, 91, 107-8, 117, 123, 128-9, 138, 140
Solskjaer, Ole Gunnar 73, 135
Sorensen, Thomas 139-40
Southampton 59, 71, 75, 85, 89, 93, 120, 145
Southend United 7, 35
Speed, Gary 19, 43, 57, 60-1, 63, 89, 108, 115, 135
Srnicek, Pavel 35
Stoke City 16, 93
Strachan, Gordon 85
Sunderland AFC 12, 23-4, 30, 36-7, 47, 49-53, 57, 58, 78, 87, 91, 93-4, 96-7, 104, 110-11, 113, 118, 120-1, 123-4, 126-7, 136, 138-40, 144-5, 147-8, 153, 155
Taylor, Bob 146
Taylor, Martin 60
Texaco Cup 94
Thomas, Andy 47
Thompson, Phil 90
Tomasson, Jon Dahl 23
Tottenham Hotspur 22, 45, 88-9, 98, 101
Townsend, Andy 32
Tranmere Rovers 7
Trezugeut, David 55

UEFA Cup 41, 68-9, 94, 113, 126, 128
Ujpesti Doza 154
Unsworth, David 67, 79, 134
Upson, Mathew 142
Van Der Sar, Edwin 85
Van Nistelrooy, Ruud 72-3, 111, 135
Vancouver Royals 113
Venables, Terry 32, 48, 99
Viana, Hugo 10, 20, 33, 39, 67, 69, 72, 117, 130, 137, 142, 146
Viduka, Mark 48
Viera, Patrick 34, 68, 107
Vieri, Christian 74, 123-4, 126
Waddle, Chris 13-14, 45, 99
Watson, Steve 67
West Bromwich Albion 56-7, 63, 145-7, 151
West Ham United 31, 33, 37, 41, 93, 96-7, 101, 142, 145, 147
Wharton, Kenny 45
Wilkinson, Howard 57, 120
Wiltord, Sylvain 68, 107
Winter, Jeff 102, 112, 118, 138
Wolverhampton Wanderers 28, 92-3, 101, 134, 149
Woodgate, Jonathan 99-100, 102, 106, 114-15, 117, 134, 146
World Cup 10-11, 30, 127, 153
Worthington Cup 56, 67, 75
Wrexham FC 16
Wright, Derek 127
Wright, Ian 86
Wright, Richard 67, 79
Yobo, Joseph 79
Zenith Data Systems Cup 7
Zola, Gianfranco 48